MW01264340

FINDING YOUR PLACE IN GOD'S ETERNAL PURPOSE

FINDING
YOUR PLACE
IN GOD'S
ETERNAL
PURPOSE

You Have Been Designed
to Reveal His Glory

LOREN COVARRUBIAS

Call from the Mountain Media
4453 Clintonville Road
Waterford, MI 48329

Finding Your Place in God's Eternal Purpose
Published by Call from the Mountain Media
Print Division
4453 Clintonville Road
Waterford, MI 48329

Unless otherwise identified, scripture references are New King James Version (NKJV) © 1982 by Thomas Nelson, Inc.

Additional emphasis in the scripture quotations through bolding reflect the author's added emphasis.

ISBN 978-0-9832084-1-9

Cover design by Grey Christian
http://www.greychristian.com/

Printed in the United States of America
2012

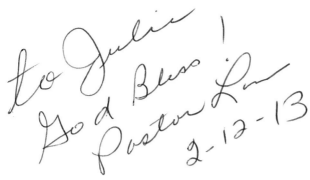

To Julie!
God Bless
Pastor [—]
2-12-13

DEDICATION

I would like to dedicate this book to all the dedicated members and staff of Mt Zion. After 35 years of following the voice of God, one thing I know without a doubt, is that all success requires a faithful God and a dedicated people willing to follow the voice of God through a person. I have many people who have been a part of my walk for the full 35 years of service! What an amazing blessing to find dedicated people. In this day and age, people seem to lack the moorings of true dedication and purpose, especially over the long haul. Without the pressure of culture keeping us in check, it will only be personal character that will hold people to the long term commitment necessary for true success in ministry. Jesus spoke of this when talking about His return, and I think it is a good question for people to ask in these latter days of time.

> *And shall God not avenge His own elect who cry out day and night to Him, though **He bears long with them?** I tell you that He will avenge them speedily. Nevertheless, when the Son of Man comes, **will He really find faith on the earth?*** (Luke 18:7)

ACKNOWLEDGMENTS

I would like to acknowledge the Covarrubias family for all of their support throughout my life and ministry. Since I was a child, my family, including Dad, Mom, and siblings, has always been there to offer support and help. When I began the work of the ministry, there they were at my side. Jesus said a prophet is not without honor save in his own family and country. My family defied that typical response by giving me honor and support all along the way. Thank You!

Contents

Contents

INTRODUCTION

We are living in a time of tremendous change. In many ways, civilization is advancing at a rapid pace. In other ways, it appears we are crumbling at the very foundations of our society. Technology and other advancements are lifting the bar of our expectations and hopes; yet, our moral uncertainty puts our whole civilization at risk. In the midst of this confusing time, I believe God is speaking clearly to the church: It is time to take your place of influence in the world. We are called to be light and salt. As light, we are to give alternatives to the secular course of life; as salt, we are to impact or influence our world for the good. To face the challenges of our present time, we need to go to a higher level of maturity. For me, it is like the time when God came to Abraham after 30 years of walking by faith and said: *"I am the Almighty God; walk before me, and be perfect."* We need to see God as He is, and we must become what He has called us to be.

For Abram and Sarai, it was time to become Abraham and Sarah. It was time to reach their perfect or completed place where they would be what God had destined them to be. In that place, the child of promise, Isaac, could be born. It would not just be the time of promises hoped for but the time for the promised to come to birth. Isaac means laughter, and for the couple of faith it would be a time of great rejoicing! They would have to get beyond themselves to go to this place, but it would certainly be worth the effort. God is calling us to go through a time of transition that will be difficult but one worth the effort. It is time to go into the "Promised Land."

To get to where God wants us, we must allow change to come into our lives and our mindsets. Abraham actually resisted the change because it seemed so far beyond him, but he ultimately submitted to God. This book is a call to the place above our human ability, a call to the place God has for us. It will be the place of God's "eternal purpose." It is an obtainable place but a place we can only reach by faith.

One of the greatest hindrances to faith is our human and religious traditions that strangle the power of God. When Jesus Christ came to the house of Israel, He was the fulfillment of the Father's purpose and the hope of the people. Yet when He came, they did not receive Him or His message. Jesus told them that they made the Word of God void by their traditions. Jesus was telling them that their mindsets hindered the Word operating in them. Their traditions did not make the purpose of God void; it only voided their ability to operate according to the Word of God. There was and always will be a people who will open themselves to the Word of God because His Word can never return to Him void but will always accomplish His purpose. The question is: Will we be the people who will allow God's Word to take root in us to bring forth the promise of God to our generation?

In 1978, I started the church I now pastor. The vision, from the beginning, was to become a church of God's Word. I wanted a church like the church spoken of in the Scripture as a glorious bride not having spot or wrinkle, representing a bride who has made herself ready for the marriage supper of the Lamb. To be ready, the bride must go on to maturity or the completion spoken of in the Scripture and demonstrated through the life of Abraham and Sarah, the patriarchs of our faith. Over the years, I realized there were mindsets and traditions we had that hindered this journey. They were traditions not based on the Word of God but the opinions of man. These concepts involve who we are and God's eternal plan for us. In order for us to reach our destiny, we must understand what our destiny is and how God intends to accomplish it in us. We must also have a clearer perception as to how God works. Many times we have put our expectations of God in the box of our own human perception and have hindered ourselves in the process.

There are some traditions I will challenge in this book, traditions that will hinder us from reaching our destiny in God. The first major tradition is the "fall of man." The idea that man fell in the garden of Eden rather than just sinned, has made the church a people always looking backward. We are always looking back to return to something rather than seeing our destiny in front of us. The concept of the "fall of man" later led to the doctrine of "total depravity." Together these concepts make our hope of reaching our God given destiny a hope impossible to believe or achieve. Secondly, we have seen the tree of knowledge of good and evil as only a test of man's obedience. The concept of the fall generating the test of man's obedience, encourages us to believe man was created to be simple and obedient rather than what God declared His intent to be. God created us in His image and likeness so we would be fruitful, multiply, and fill up the earth. We were created to be mature sons, not little children. This development comes through a process of our relationship with God. As it was for Abraham so it is for us. We are being called to take another step in our journey to God's destiny for us.

As the Lord began to show me these things by the Holy Spirit, I felt compelled to go back into church doctrine. I knew that if it was the truth it would be preserved in church history. I found out these three concepts were indeed preserved in the Eastern Church traditions. The Eastern Church teaches the doctrine of "theosis," the process by which we become more like God in union with Him. They do not see the fall as we Western Christians do. Instead, they see the sin of man resulting in an *anthro*centic or man centered world rather than a *theo*centric or God centered one. The world was changed, but man was not corrupted by it. As a result, we need to put God back into proper perspective in our life and grow in union with Him. The Eastern concept of the tree of knowledge of good and evil is that it represented a choice to learn through observation or participation. This choice is still before us today. It would seem strange for Western Christians to open themselves up to what they consider a new concept; but we must understand, as the church has moved forward over the years, it is typical for God to shine new light on hidden truths. Why does God operate in this manner? God is a God of appointed times. We must be open to recognize God's appointed times. We can see new perspectives on these concepts in the great awakening of the 1800s, not fully clarified but certainly challenged, by the call to perfection and sanctification in the moves of God for those times.

Over time, my observations have shown truth always has two sides to it. Even the creation, reveals God's plan to involve the polarity of forces, positive and negative for example, as the basis of creation. The Bible is filled with seemingly contradictory sides of the truth. The church believes God to be one and also three. Jesus is man, and He is God. These truths because they are contradictory have often been the source of debate and strife, and it is difficult for the human mind to put them together. The mystery of God is above our human comprehension, so rather than embrace the fullness of truth, we usually take sides. While counseling through the years, I have found you must hear both sides to know the truth; and it is true concerning the Word of God.

This is a time when as Christians we must open our eyes to see the truths God has deposited in the greater body of Christ and to be open to the day of joining when God will begin to put the parts of the puzzle of His hidden wisdom together. The house of Israel became two: Israel and Judah. The early church divided into two: the Western and Eastern. The Western Church divided into two: the catholic and protestant. The Protestants separated into the Calvinists and the Armenians. Could this now be the time of the joining of the twos to make one? We shouldn't be taking sides but expanding ourselves to receive the whole truth. This is the day of the joining.

> *Again the word of the LORD came to me, saying, "As for you, son of man, take a stick for yourself and write on it: 'For Judah and for the children of Israel, his companions.' Then take another stick and write on it, 'For Joseph, the stick of*

Ephraim, and for all the house of Israel, his companions.'
Then join them one to another for yourself into one stick, and
they will become one in your hand. (Ezekiel 37:15-17)

Please read this book with an open mind and heart, and let God speak to you through these words. Don't be afraid to examine your beliefs, but let God expand you to see beyond your ability so that like Abraham and Sarah you also can be a person with the promise fulfilled!

Chapter One

WHERE DOES GOD'S PLAN
BEGIN FOR YOU?

However, we speak wisdom among those who are mature, yet not the wisdom of this age, nor of the rulers of this age, who are coming to nothing. But we speak the wisdom of God in a mystery, the hidden wisdom which God ordained before the ages for our glory, (1 Corinthians 2:6-7)

When we contemplate the purpose of God from the beginning, we need to understand that the beginning was long before the creation of the earth and the creation of man. God is an eternal God with an eternal purpose, and now He is calling us to both participate and understand His plan and purpose for us. It is time for us to become mature in our understanding so we can participate in the plan of God from a position of maturity and not from a position of immaturity. It is time to quit being children in our understanding but mature sons of the Most High God. The Scriptures involve the unfolding plan of God for man. Church history has continued this unfolding through the revelation and understanding God has continually given to us. It is time for a new level of maturity and with this maturity a new level of understanding. I am writing this book to encourage you in your pursuit of God's purpose for your life and to encourage you to see God's purpose, not just from the human perspective but from God's.

When the New Testament was given by the Holy Spirit, the authors made known to us the revelation of the mystery of God contained in the Old Testament. I remember hearing a preacher say, "The Old Testament is the will of God concealed, and the New Testament is the will of God revealed." In a sense, this is true in that many things were concealed until an appointed time; but the Scriptures continue to unfold the plan of God over time. The coming of Christ and New Testament revelations made the plan much more clear, but we can have further revelation as God is bringing us to a greater level of maturity. The Scriptures tell us that when maturity or completeness comes, our partial understanding will become more complete.

> *For we know in part and we prophesy in part. But when that which is perfect has come, then that which is in part will be done away. When I was a child, I spoke as a child, I understood as a child, I thought as a child; but when I became a man, I put away childish things.* (1 Corinthians 13:9-11)

God's eternal plan had a beginning, and it has an end. God is Alpha and Omega, the Beginning and the End, the First and the Last. History revolves around God and His purpose, and in order to relate to what God is doing we must understand this. God didn't seek our advice in the beginning, and He isn't looking for it now. We must see God establishes His purpose within Himself, then, He makes known His purpose to us and invites us to participate in it. His purpose revolves around Jesus Christ, and we must see ourselves in relationship to Him.

> *having made known to us the mystery of His will, according to His good pleasure which He purposed in Himself, that in the dispensation of the fullness of the times He might gather together in one all things in Christ, both which are in heaven and which are on earth—in Him. In Him also we have obtained an inheritance, being predestined according to the purpose of Him who works all things according to the counsel of His will, that we who first trusted in Christ should be to the praise of His glory.* (Ephesians 1: 9-12)

Our inheritance and our purpose must be found in Christ. When we first come to Jesus Christ, we place our trust in His salvation; but we have to also understand we must *be to the praise of His glory."* As you read this book, you will note that God is taking us somewhere with Him. Christianity is not static or passive. We are called to move forward in God, to be an integral part of His plan. Those of us who know Christ should see ourselves as people appointed out of eternity for eternity. Just think, before the foundation of the world you were planned and appointed by God!

> *Blessed be the God and Father of our Lord Jesus Christ, who has blessed us with every spiritual blessing in the heavenly places in Christ, just* **as He chose us in Him before the foundation of the world,** *that we should be holy and without blame before Him in love, having predestined us to adoption as sons by Jesus Christ to Himself, according to the good pleasure of His will, to the praise of the glory of His grace, by which He made us accepted in the Beloved.* (Ephesians 1:3-6)

Just as we need to see the eternal purpose of God for ourselves, we must also see that His purpose does not end with us as individuals. The eternal purpose we have been called to has brought us out of our individual aspirations to God's. This brings us to the second aspect of God's intention. The aspiration of God is not just for the glory of individuals but for the calling together of all things in Jesus Christ. Once we have been committed to our individual destiny, we must get beyond our personal aspirations to be joined fully to Jesus Christ. This destiny calls us to be a part of the eternal hope of God and His Christ through the church. Jesus Christ and His church are one, so you cannot say you are joined to one and not the other.

> *and to make all see what is the fellowship of the mystery, which from the beginning of the ages has been hidden in God who created all things through Jesus Christ; to the intent that now the manifold wisdom of God might be made known by the church to the principalities and powers in the heavenly*

places, according to the eternal purpose which He accom-
plished in Christ Jesus our Lord, (Ephesians 3:9-11)

The word "church" in its original meaning literally is the "called out ones" or the "calling together." The church is the gathering place of the called out ones of God. Those of us who are called, need to understand the two aspects of our calling. First, as individuals we are called out from the world to God to become the children of God. Secondly, as children of God we are called to follow the steps of Jesus Christ who gave His life for the church.

Husbands, love your wives, just as Christ also loved the
church and gave Himself for her, that He might sanctify and
cleanse her with the washing of water by the word, that He
might present her to Himself a glorious church , not having
spot or wrinkle or any such thing, but that she should be holy
and without blemish. (Ephesians 5:25-27)

These Scriptures in Ephesians demonstrate the unity of God's purpose from the beginning and tell us it was shrouded in mystery before the appointed time. To fully comprehend the purpose of God, we need the spirit of revelation so we can fully appreciate the hidden mystery of God. The mystery is hidden in the natural order God has set up. This order is demonstrated here in Ephesians when describing God's plan and purpose for mankind from the beginning.

When reading the story of Genesis concerning the creation of man, we have the creation story itself; but we also see the deeper spiritual aspect God wants to convey about His eternal plan. We know when God created Adam, the first man, He stated this man was incomplete. He needed a helper suitable for Him to fulfill his purpose. This is why Eve was created, to help Adam fulfill his purpose. When we get to the New Testament, the deeper meaning God wants to convey is how this story reveals His plan for the church as the bride of Christ. Jesus Christ came to establish a new order. He came as the "Last Adam" who would fulfill the Father's purpose and establish the church, which would consist of those who would, as His bride, help fulfill this purpose.

> *So husbands ought to love their own wives as their own bodies; he who loves his wife loves himself. For no one ever hated his own flesh, but nourishes and cherishes it, just as the Lord does the church. For we are members of His body, of His flesh and of His bones. "For this reason a man shall leave his father and mother and be joined to his wife, and the two shall become one flesh." This is a great mystery, but I speak concerning Christ and the church.* (Ephesians 5:28-32)

Did you ever wonder why the story of the temptation of the tree of knowledge of good and evil centered around Eve and not Adam? In the story, Adam was the one given the charge of responsibility in the garden of Eden while Eve was created as his helper. Yet, when Eve is beguiled by the serpent, Adam simply eats of the tree without much involvement in the story. With the revelation of the mystery in Ephesians, it is clear it was the story of Christ and the church. Jesus Christ, as the last Adam, completely fulfilled His purpose. The question is: Will He find a bride willing to take her place and become the helper she was intended to be? This is why one has to look for the deeper clues of the prophetic to see that in this story God was actually foretelling of a future time. In the future time, the bride of Christ would fully take her place and be the agent God would use to fully overcome the power of the enemy in order to become the victorious bride of Christ!

> *So the LORD God said to the serpent: "Because you have done this, You are cursed more than all cattle, And more than every beast of the field; On your belly you shall go, And you shall eat dust All the days of your life. And **I will put enmity Between you and the woman**, And between your seed and her Seed; **He shall bruise your head, And you shall bruise His heel.**"* (Genesis 3:14-15)

It is evident from these passages that Christ will return for both a glorious and victorious bride. When you see this, it will change your perspective on many of the Scriptures and your point of view concerning where the world is heading. God's intention is that His church would be a shining light to the world as a witness. Our witness of the power of God is not just verbal but visual. God intends us to be a visible witness of His power and glory working in the earth and in His people. The vision of my life, as a pastor, is for the church to become everything the Father says and intends it to be. I fully expect that in the last days the church will be a glorious and shining light that will demonstrate the glory and light of God to the nations. I believe this because I believe in the God with an eternal purpose.

> *Now **it shall come to pass in the latter days That the mountain of the LORD's house Shall be established on the top of the mountains,** And shall be exalted above the hills; **And all nations shall flow to it.** Many people shall come and say, "Come, and let us go up to the mountain of the LORD, To the house of the God of Jacob; He will teach us His ways, And we shall walk in His paths." For out of Zion shall go forth the law, And the word of the LORD from Jerusalem.* (Isaiah 2:2-3)

Now going back to the beginning, we must also see the full implication of God's purpose for mankind. To do this, we must take in the context of chapter 1 of Genesis. When God first created mankind, He created us in His own image and likeness with a call for dominion over His creation.

> *Then God said, "**Let Us make man in Our image, according to Our likeness;** let them have dominion over the fish of the sea, over the birds of the air, and over the cattle, over all the earth and over every creeping thing that creeps on the earth." So God created man in His own image; in the image of God He created him; male and female He created them. Then God blessed them, and God said to them, "**Be fruitful and multi-***

WHERE DOES GOD'S PLAN BEGIN FOR YOU?

ply; fill the earth and subdue it; have dominion over the fish
of the sea, over the birds of the air, and over every living thing
that moves on the earth." (Genesis 1:26-28)

The first and perhaps more important part of this eternal plan
is God's intent for us individually. It is more important only because
the total will be a composite of the individual parts, so for the
church to excel we need to see our individual purpose. This individual purpose has to do with the work of God in each and every
one of us to make us into the person He has called us to be so we
can indeed fulfill our eternal purpose. This work has to do with us
conforming to the person we are in Christ Jesus so that He can be
the firstborn, as the "Last Adam," raising up the seed of God in the
earth. This concept is fully endorsed by the apostle Paul as the purpose for God calling us and working in each of our lives.

> *And we know that all things work together for good to those
> who love God, to those who are the called according to His
> purpose. For whom He foreknew, He also **predestined to be
> conformed to the image of His Son, that He might be the
> firstborn among many brethren.** Moreover whom He pre-
> destined, these He also called; whom He called, these He also
> justified; and whom He justified, these **He also glorified.** (Ro-
> mans 8:28-30)*

With this in mind, we see how important it will be to change
our perspective on how we approach and proclaim the message of
the kingdom of God. The goal of the gospel is not to find "souls"
to fill up heaven but to birth sons who will grow into maturity and
become everything the Father has purposed us to be. We are called
and justified, but did you also know you were destined to glory? It
is when we move forward to our destiny of glory individually that
the church will fulfill her mission as the glorious bride in the earth.
If we fail to see the eternal purpose, we will certainly fail to preach
the message God wants conveyed to the earth. Not only must this
message be conveyed to the earth, both by proclamation and

demonstration, but the(church must become the house of the Father.)The church must(be able to both birth and equip the people of God.)It is time for us to change our perspective on God and His purpose so we can fully participate in His plan.

Now, we can see very clearly God's intent from the beginning of time. This intent is not always clearly evident because God reveals everything in the appointed time. The appointed time is when God is ready to move everything another step forward. The appointed time is when He has prepared a people and an environment capable of sustaining and carrying out His purpose. This is why we need to understand God has an appointed purpose, eternal in scope, but progressive in motion. This is also why we need to carefully consider what God is speaking in the present tense so that we can open ourselves to the plan of God in our time. This is only possible by giving heed to the prophetic voice that is declaring the present truth of our time. Like the apostles and people in the time of Christ who received and declared the present truth, we need to do the same in our time.

> *Therefore, brethren, be even more diligent to make your call and election sure, for if you do these things you will never stumble; for so an entrance will be supplied to you abundantly into the everlasting kingdom of our Lord and Savior Jesus Christ. For this reason I will not be negligent to remind you always of these things, though you know and are established in the present truth.* (2 Peter 1:10-12)

The abundant entrance is made possible by responding to the voice of the prophets.

> *So they rose early in the morning and went out into the Wilderness of Tekoa; and as they went out, Jehoshaphat stood and said, "Hear me, O Judah and you inhabitants of Jerusalem: Believe in the LORD your God, and you shall be established; believe His prophets, and you shall prosper.* (2 Chronicles 20:20)

What is the <u>ministry of a prophet</u>? The <u>prophet gives insight</u> <u>into the deeper spiritual aspect of the Word and what is happening</u> <u>in the world today</u>. This was the function of the apostle Paul in the Scriptures as he declared the Word and prayed for the Ephesian church that they would be enlightened to see the deeper truth of God. He knew it would only be through enlightenment that they would be able to see and have hope for the calling of Christ.

> *do not cease to give thanks for you, making mention of you in my prayers: that the God of our Lord Jesus Christ, the Father of glory, may give to you the spirit of wisdom and revelation in the knowledge of Him, the eyes of your understanding being enlightened; that you may know what is the hope of His calling, what are the riches of the glory of His inheritance in the saints, and what is the exceeding greatness of His power toward us who believe, according to the working of His mighty power* (Ephesians 1:16-19)

We need prophetic ministry. In recent years, the Pentecostals and charismatic Christians have recognized the need for this important ministry. When you understand God's eternal purpose at work, you will easily see how ministries do not need our recognition in order to operate. This prophetic ministry has been at work all along even when not recognized as such. Throughout the history of man, God has raised up people to declare a relevant word for the time, calling the people of God to a higher purpose than life as they were living it. The people of the Old Testament recognized prophets as did the early church.

Now, we are once again seeing prophecy in many circles; but through the history of the church, God has raised up people to bring fresh light on the Scriptures to take us to a higher plane of understanding and practice. This was easily seen when Martin Luther rose up to bring the church to a higher plane during the Reformation followed by many others in later years. Most denominations and people groups formed, since the time of the Reformation, are the result of "prophetic spokesmen" God raised up to take His people to a higher plane. Unfortunately, we have typically taken on these new identities without hearing the other relevant voices God wanted to raise up to continue the process of His eternal purpose. As you read this book, ask God to give you the spirit of enlightenment and understanding so you will be able to manifest the glory of God in this generation.

Not only do we need a full understanding of the purpose of God, we also need to fully see Him. It is only when we see Him as He is that we will fully comprehend His purpose. The unfolding of God's purpose has also been an unfolding of who He is. Remember, God's plan and purpose does not change; it is only our perception of His purpose that will change. This is also true of God. God does not change.

> *For I am the LORD, I do not change; Therefore you are not consumed, O sons of Jacob.* (Malachi 3:6)

Many people have a God who changes with the times. This is often the impression people have about God based on the dramatic change from the Old Testament to the New Testament. Jesus Christ came to change our perception of God and His purpose. Jesus Christ came to show us that the revelation of God is ongoing, but it is the same God. Jesus Christ was the very person worshipped and followed by the Old Testament people of God, although they were not aware of who He was.

> *You search the Scriptures, for in them you think you have eternal life; and these are they which testify of Me. But you are not willing to come to Me that you may have life.* (John 5:39-40)

When Jesus Christ was so bold as to declare the consistency of the revelation of God in Him, they wanted to kill Him.

> *Your father Abraham rejoiced to see My day, and he saw it and was glad." Then the Jews said to Him, "You are not yet fifty years old, and have You seen Abraham?" Jesus said to them, "Most assuredly, I say to you, before Abraham was, I*

AM." Then they took up stones to throw at Him . . . (John 8:56-59)

What angered them the most is when He called Himself the "I AM." This was truly saying He was the God who had revealed Himself throughout the ages, and they refused to hear it. We need to have a progressive revelation of God; yet, at the same time make sure we are not changing God to fit our times. Jesus Christ was the one who met Moses at the burning bush and now had come to take His people further.

> *And God said to Moses, "I AM WHO I AM." And He said, "Thus you shall say to the children of Israel, 'I AM has sent me to you.'" Moreover God said to Moses, "Thus you shall say to the children of Israel: 'The LORD God of your fathers, the God of Abraham, the God of Isaac, and the God of Jacob, has sent me to you. This is My name forever, and this is My memorial to all generations.'* (Exodus 3:14-15)

When God met Moses, He was adamant to declare He was who He was, not who we want Him to be. However, just as He was the God of Abraham, Isaac, and Jacob; He is also our God today. Just as He revealed Himself in an ongoing fashion to produce change and purpose in the life of the patriarchs, He wants to reveal Himself more fully to us so we can be all He has intended us to be. God is once again speaking and calling to His people to move forward. Remember the story of Jesus Christ. When He came to His own, they chose their traditions and patterns from the past rather than listening clearly to the message. Because of this, what was meant for them had to go to someone else. Will you turn down what God has for you in this day? Will you let God's blessing go to someone else? There will be someone willing if you are not!

> *He was in the world, and the world was made through Him, and the world did not know Him. He came to His own, and His own did not receive Him. But as many as received Him, to them He gave the right to become children of God, to those*

who believe in His name: who were born, not of blood, nor of the will of the flesh, nor of the will of man, but of God. (John 1:10-13)

This is why it is important to see the consistency of the revelation of God. In the beginning there was God, the initiator, the Father. When the Father spoke, the Word went forth to create. This was Jesus Christ, the Son, who made all things. The Holy Spirit was also present in the creation, hovering over the face of the waters, as the brooding mind of God contemplating His actions. They still operate in this way today.

But God has revealed them to us through His Spirit. For the Spirit searches all things, yes, the deep things of God. For what man knows the things of a man except the spirit of the man which is in him? Even so no one knows the things of God except the Spirit of God. (1 Corinthians 2:10-11)

As we read the creation account, we see a very important concept God wanted to reveal concerning Himself that is a major factor in our understanding of God and history. It is the revelation of the Sabbath rest instituted in chapter 2 of the book of Genesis.

Thus the heavens and the earth, and all the host of them, were finished. And on the seventh day God ended His work which He had done, and He rested on the seventh day from all His work which He had done. Then God blessed the seventh day and sanctified it, because in it He rested from all His work which God had created and made. (Genesis 2:1-3)

Throughout the time of the law and the prophets, God emphasized the need to honor the Sabbath. Under the law, breaking the law of the Sabbath was punishable by death. The Sabbath was not just a part of the weekly order but was included in other festivities to emphasize this important principle. For the people, the Sabbath offers an opportunity to rest, which is very important to our health.(Ceasing from our labors also gives us an opportunity to meditate upon God and His Word, which not only gives us a better relationship with God but offers the blessing of a good life.⟩

> *This Book of the Law shall not depart from your mouth, but you shall meditate in it day and night, that you may observe to do according to all that is written in it. For then you will make your way prosperous, and then you will have good success.* (Joshua 1: 8)

What it reveals about God is the most important message in the Sabbath. The ultimate revelation of the Sabbath is the understanding that not only did God create all things but He designed all things to ultimately fulfill His purpose. He set in motion an unfolding purpose that will absolutely come to pass.

> *For we who have believed do enter that rest, as He has said: "So I swore in My wrath, 'They shall not enter My rest,'" although the works were finished from the foundation of the world. For He has spoken in a certain place of the seventh day in this way: "And God rested on the seventh day from all His works"; There remains therefore a rest for the people of God. For he who has entered His rest has himself also ceased from his works as God did from His.* (Hebrews 4: 3-4 & 9-10)

God didn't just take a day off. He has ceased from His labor for the work was finished from the foundation of the world. In this day, we, the people of God, must enter the rest of the "finished work," a work finished since the foundation of the world! Verse seven of this reference says: *"again He designates a certain day, saying in David, "Today," after such a long time, as it has been said: "Today, if you will hear His voice, Do not harden your hearts."* I believe this is one of those "today" times when God wants us to open our hearts to a fresh outpouring of His presence and a fresh understanding of His Word so we can move to another plane in our walk with Him and in our witness to the world. As you read this book, pray also that the eyes of your understanding would be opened that you would see the hope of your calling in Christ.

In Summary

Christianity is not static or passive. It is progressive. Once we are committed to our individual destiny, we must get beyond our personal aspirations to be joined to Jesus Christ through the church. God's intention is for His church to be a shining light to the world as a witness of His power. God intends us to be a visible witness of His power and glory working in the earth and in His people.

For the church to excel we need to see our individual purpose and see how each individual part fits into the whole to accomplish His purpose. To fully comprehend the purpose of God, we need the spirit of revelation so we can fully appreciate the hidden mystery of God. The mystery is hidden in the natural order God has set up. As we see the mystery unfold, we will see God's intent for us to become His glorious bride who will overcome the power of the enemy. The goal of the gospel is not to find "souls" to fill up heaven but to birth sons who will grow into maturity and become everything the Father has purposed us to be. God has an appointed purpose, eternal in scope, but progressive in motion.

We must have a revelation of who God is. The unfolding of God's purpose has also been an unfolding of who He is. God does not change. Jesus Christ came to show us that the revelation of God is ongoing, but it is the same God.

God has ceased from His labor for the work was finished from the foundation of the world. God wants His people to enter into the "rest" of the finished work. This can only happen when we understand who God is and see the hope of our calling in Christ.

Chapter Two

Is God Trying to Control You?

When I consider Your heavens, the work of Your fingers, The moon and the stars, which You have ordained, What is man that You are mindful of him, And the son of man that You visit him? You have made him to have dominion over the works of Your hands; You have put all things under his feet. (Psalm 8:3-6)

Going into chapter 3 of the book of Genesis, we see Adam and Eve facing their first test. After God created man and gave him dominion of His creation, He placed him in a garden He had planted for him. The garden of Eden was a place obviously endowed in a manner the name implied. The word "Eden" means voluptuous living or delightful land. It was a garden God planted for mankind. The prophet Ezekiel called it "God's Garden." Truly God wanted to bless this creature, man.

Once placed in the garden of Eden, Adam was told he could eat of all the trees of the garden except the tree of the knowledge of good and evil. Looking at the task before him, it was obvious man needed help. His responsibility was not one he could face alone. God created a helper that was also made after His image and likeness. God created the helper from Adam and brought her to him. He called her name *woman*, for she was taken out of man. The words "helper suitable for him" in the original context mean both an aide and one who stands opposite. Woman represents a second part of man now in another. From this point forward, man would have to see his need not just to stand alone but to be joined to others.

One day Eve, apparently within eyesight of the tree of knowledge of good and evil, is tempted by the serpent to disobey God and eat of the forbidden tree. Eve not only disobeys God but she also gives the fruit to her husband. He also eats putting them in direct opposition to the word of God. This failure and the weakness displayed by man throughout history would certainly be the motivation of the question of the Psalmist: "Who is man that God would be mindful of him?" Why would God put such a great responsibility and honor upon mankind when we seem so ill equipped to handle the responsibility God has given us?

When the serpent tempts Eve, his first course of action is to get her to question God's motivation. He says: *"You will not surely die. For God knows that in the day you eat of it your eyes will be opened, and you will be like God, knowing good and evil."* This statement implies God's plan is to keep man simple and under His control so God can use man for His own selfish pleasure.

How different this is from God's true intent. God had created man in His image and likeness so he could take dominion of all His works. God's plan was not to control but to supervise. He had a long range plan of responsibility and blessing intended for us; but as is often true today, we think we will be better off if we seize control of our lives and chart our own course. The serpent here is someone who is not fully explained in this text. It isn't until the book of the Revelation we are explicitly informed this is the devil or satan.

> So the great dragon was cast out, **that serpent of old, called the Devil and Satan,** who deceives the whole world; he was cast to the earth, and his angels were cast out with him. (Revelation 12:9)

The devil is the deceiver. The word ("devil" means accuser, and the name satan means adversary;) and this is what he does. In this case, he was actually accusing God of being self-centered and controlling, two lies still prevalent in the people of God today. We not only accept these lies we have encompassed them in our theology much to our detriment. It is time to expose this lie and allow

God to be who He really is. It is time for the people of God to move forward and become all He has called us to be!

When Eve started down the road to self-centered motivation and desires, a whole new world opened. Although it may appear God has placed temptation before them, the Scripture is very clear where this road begins.

> *Let no one say when he is tempted, "I am tempted by God"; for God cannot be tempted by evil, nor does He Himself tempt anyone. But each one is tempted when he is drawn away by his own desires and enticed. Then, when desire has conceived, it gives birth to sin; and sin, when it is full-grown, brings forth death.* (James 1:13-15)

Although God is not the source of temptation, He is the one who offers us a choice. It is a real choice because He not only gives us a choice but He also supplies the advocate for the other side. This should not be seen as a temptation but as a real choice. As we walk the road of faith, we will always note that there will be someone close by advocating for us to change our mind or "think about ourselves." The serpent was obviously someone Eve felt comfortable talking to, and your advisors will be the same. Always remember: truth comes from God. Although there may be many opinions offered to you, be sure you are following God and not the voice of human reason.

> *Certainly not! Indeed, let **God be true but every man a liar.** As it is written: "That You may be justified in Your words, And may overcome when You are judged."* (Romans 3:4)

God is a God of truth, and in the end even his judgments will be for our justification. When God is involved, we should always be looking for His "good plan" leading to our justification. It is even true in this story when you see it as a part of God's eternal plan. Truth is not only the road of God but truth will always prevail in the end. The truth of this story is God started the work, and He will finish the work.

After listening to the wrong advice, Eve has a different perspective on her choices. Oh how careful we need to be when it comes to who and what we are listening to. Once she is convinced she has to chart her own course, she sees the tree of knowledge of good and evil from the perspective of human desire, and it looks very good.

> *So when the woman saw that the tree was good for food, that it was pleasant to the eyes, and a tree desirable to make one wise, she took of its fruit and ate. She also gave to her husband with her, and he ate. (Genesis 3:6)*

Note how closely this resembles the description of the world.

> *Do not love the world or the things in the world. If anyone loves the world, the love of the Father is not in him. For all that is in the world — the lust of the flesh, the lust of the eyes, and the pride of life — is not of the Father but is of the world. And the world is passing away, and the lust of it; but he who does the will of God abides forever. (1 John 2:15-17)*

The world is the biblical term to describe the order and attraction outside the will of God enticing man to fulfill his own desire. Our modern world has a much bigger presence, but the allure and strength is not any different than it was in the garden of Eden. Just as it was in the garden, so it is today. We are called to obey God and take our proper place of authority. The real conflict is not external but internal. Will we trust God and go His way, or will we try to take control and go our own way? The setting of the garden is a picture of the long term plan. God would give mankind choices and advocates for the other side, so we would not only learn to follow God but would learn wisdom in the process.

We must, however, understand it isn't just a choice of obedience. God's end game is not obedient people but mature sons. Obedience sets us on the course, but it is not the end. When we understand this, it changes the whole perspective on how we will view God, ourselves, and the world we live in. The church has for too long been controlled by immature thinking. Our idea is God wants to keep us simple and obedient while He controls the world. Keeping people simple is the governing principle of the Christian church and has made us unable to produce the true sons of God in the earth. The devil's lie was that God wanted to keep us from information so we would not be wise enough to disobey or question God. As the plan of God unfolds, we will see God does not want us to be children in actions or understanding, but He wants us to be mature.

> *Brethren, do not be children in understanding; however, in malice be babes, but in understanding be mature.* (1 Corinthians 14:20)

God wants us to become as little children. It is only when we humble ourselves in this fashion we will be able to fulfill our Father's purpose.

> *Assuredly, I say to you, whoever does not receive the kingdom of God as a little child will by no means enter it.* (Luke 18:17)

Although we must enter with the humility of a child, God then wants us to grow and develop in understanding. Humility will give us the power to live with God as the center of our lives and not our own desires and efforts. From this point, we can grow into the fullness of what God has for us.

It is obvious from the initial story of creation that God does not want us to remain children. The fact that adversity is allowed lets us see how God wants to bring us to a place of responsibility. Some people teach the devil was a fallen angel that kind of snuck into this story or that he was a leftover from a previous time who just happened to be there trying to spoil God's plan for man. I have even heard tell that the devil was the most powerful force on the planet; hence, he sought to circumvent God's plan for man because he was jealous. These scenarios are mostly conjecture and have very little biblical evidence. I wrote a whole book on this subject called *Why is the Devil in My Garden?* It is important we understand that since God is the God Most High, Creator of heaven and earth that the only way the devil could be here is by divine design. His being was obviously designed and planned by God.

> *Now the **serpent was more cunning** than any beast of the field which the LORD God had made. And he said to the woman, "Has God indeed said, 'You shall not eat of every tree of the garden'?"* (Genesis 3:1)

If God makes something, I am sure it is no surprise to Him the purpose and the ability of the creature and what impact it can have on His creation. After the Lord comes to look into the situation, when Adam and Eve disobeyed Him, He makes an announcement. The seed of the woman would eventually defeat the power of the devil. This prophecy was fulfilled in Jesus Christ.

> *He who sins is of the devil, for the devil has sinned from the beginning. For this purpose the Son of God was manifested, that He might destroy the works of the devil.* (1 John 3:8)

It was important that Jesus Christ would come from the seed of the woman because God intended for this victory to come through man. Jesus Christ came to show us a man, or human, could walk in complete fulfillment of the Father's purpose for him. The ultimate authority will be exercised by the church, as the seed of Christ and the woman. This is an allegory of the church. The ultimate victory over all things will be accomplished through the church.

> *And He put all things under His feet, and gave Him to be head over all things to the church, which is His body, the fullness of Him who fills all in all.* (Ephesians 1:22-23)

When all things are under the feet of Jesus Christ, they will be under us, for we are His body and the fullness of the plan of God.

Now the interesting aspect of this story goes back to Adam. He seems to be a minor player here because although this is a real story, the allegory, or mystery Paul spoke of in Ephesians, reveals that this story is about Christ and the church. It is interesting to understand here how God has a long term plan. Jesus Christ was always in the plan. In order for man to take the place God has for us, we certainly need to progress along the line of the divine plan. Here we need to understand the difference between the two Adams.

> *And so it is written, "The first man Adam became a living being." The last Adam became a life-giving spirit. However, the spiritual is not first, but the natural, and afterward the spiritual. The first man was of the earth, made of dust; the second Man is the Lord from heaven. As was the man of dust, so also are those who are made of dust; and as is the heavenly Man, so also are those who are heavenly.* (1 Corinthians 15:45-48)

In this story, Adam represents the human side of who we are. When God first creates man, He makes us from the dust of the earth, and we become a living being. Although God has made us, we are from the earth until we experience the second birth and are born again. When we are born again, we become partakers of the divine nature. With the spirit of Christ, we have a life-giving spirit. I like to say we are born a noun, but through Christ we become a verb. When we come into this life, we are influenced by our environment. Through the second birth, we are called to influence our environment. In the natural, we cannot have the impact on the creation we are supposed to have; but in Christ, we can truly fulfill our divine destiny. When we come to the fullness of Christ, we do become a life-giving influence. When Jesus met the woman at the well of Samaria, she seemed to be a person influenced and possibly a victim of her life experiences. When she met Jesus Christ, He told her if she would come to Him she would not only find life but it would emanate from her.

> *Jesus answered and said to her, "If you knew the gift of God, and who it is who says to you, 'Give Me a drink,' you would have asked Him, and He would have given you living water." Jesus answered and said to her, "Whoever drinks of this*

water will thirst again, but whoever drinks of the water that I shall give him will never thirst. But the water that I shall give him will become in him a fountain of water springing up into everlasting life." (John 4:10, 13-14)

After this encounter with Jesus Christ, the woman at the well literally turned her whole city around. God is seeking people of faith today that will be able to turn their world around!

In the garden of Eden, man was not equipped to fully be the agent of influence he was created to be. God knew this, but in His long range plan He would have a different expectation. Many people see this story as the fall of man. The idea was that man was created in the image and likeness of God but lost something in the garden. The Bible does not tell us this; it is only something people have assumed. When looking at this event from an eternal point of view, you can easily see what God's point of view would be. God only puts on us the expectation He has equipped us to fulfill. God had placed man in the garden, a prepared place, until the time he would be prepared to fulfill the Father's plan. Jesus Christ would not come until many years later. His coming would not be an afterthought nor a response to man's failure since Jesus Christ had an appointed time before the foundation of the world.

> *But when the fullness of the time had come, God sent forth His Son, born of a woman, born under the law, to redeem those who were under the law, that we might receive the adoption as sons. (Galatians 4:4-5)*

The Scriptures are clear that God would deal with us as children until the right time. This is true in the natural and also in the spiritual. Just as children are under the care of their parents until an appointed time, so God has appointed times for His people.

> *Now I say that the heir, as long as he is a child, does not differ at all from a slave, though he is master of all, but is under guardians and stewards until the time appointed by the father. Even so we, when we were children, were in bondage*

under the elements of the world. But when the fullness of the time had come, God sent forth His Son, born of a woman, born under the law. (Galatians 4:1-4)

This is why in the garden the issue was simply obedience. In the garden, man was not capable of anything. When we understand the times of God, we can also see how God's expectation changes according to the time. This is why, in these latter days of time, we must understand God has a greater expectation of the church. What He expected in the past is not what He expects today. This why we need this change of understanding, so that we can have a greater understanding of what God is looking for from us today.

The final point we need to discuss in this story is the issue of God's judgment of death. God had said in the day they ate of the tree of the knowledge of good and evil they would die. Now some people surmise from this that before what they call "the fall of man" death was not a part of the natural order. This is mostly based on the Scripture in the book of Romans.

Therefore, just as through one man sin entered the world, and death through sin, and thus death spread to all men, because all sinned. (Romans 5:12)

There is nothing in this story to give the impression the experience itself created some tragedy on Adam and Eve personally. The judgment of death upon them was because Adam and Eve would no longer have access to the tree of life. Without access to the tree of life, Adam and Eve would follow the natural course and die.

Then the LORD God said, "Behold, the man has become like one of Us, to know good and evil. And now, lest he put out his hand and take also of the tree of life, and eat, and live forever" — therefore the LORD God sent him out of the garden of Eden to till the ground from which he was taken. (Genesis 3:22-23)

Death was not something newly placed upon Adam and Eve. Death is a part of the natural order. What God did is take away their access to the antidote. God's pattern, we will see throughout His eternal plan, is to provide an antidote for man's human weakness. In the beginning, it was the limitation of the human being on his physical life. Without God's divine life, he would eventually die and decay. It is still true today. Without God, we go the way of the natural order; but when we partake of the life of God in Jesus Christ we will have eternal life. That is the power of the Life-Giving Spirit. The same spirit that raised Christ from the dead will do the same for us.

> *But if the Spirit of Him who raised Jesus from the dead dwells in you, He who raised Christ from the dead will also give life to your mortal bodies through His Spirit who dwells in you.* (Romans 8:11)

When we get to the end of the Scriptures, in the book of Revelation, we see the glorious picture of the end of this matter.

> *And he showed me a pure river of water of life, clear as crystal, proceeding from the throne of God and of the Lamb. In the middle of its street, and on either side of the river, was the tree of life, which bore twelve fruits, each tree yielding its fruit every month. The leaves of the tree were for the healing of the nations.* (Revelations 22:1-2)

(The tree of life has multiplied to twelve. This represents the church that will be the glorious life force of God to the nations.)As the church moves forward in our understanding of the beginning, we will also have the faith to move forward to the full understanding of the end. What was pictured in the garden became a reality in Christ. Now the reality will be consummated in the glorious church He has given His life for.

> *Along the bank of the river, on this side and that, will grow all kinds of trees used for food; their leaves will not wither, and their fruit will not fail. They will bear fruit every month,*

*because their water flows from the sanctuary. Their fruit will
be for food, and their leaves for medicine.* (Ezekiel 47:12)

In Summary

Although many people think that God is controlling, God created man in His image and likeness so man could take dominion of all God's works. God's plan was not to control but to supervise. He has a long range plan of responsibility and blessing intended for us.

The devil is a deceiver and an accuser. He perpetrated the lie that God is self-centered and controlling. God offers us a choice. By creating the devil, He even provided an advocate for the opposing side. In our choice, we must be careful who we listen to. We are called to obey God and take our proper place of authority. The real conflict is not external but internal. It isn't just a choice of obedience. God is looking for mature sons who will develop and grow in understanding so that He can give them authority. The ultimate authority will be exercised by the church, as the seed of Christ and the woman.

When we come to the fullness of Christ, we become a life giving influence. We start with simple obedience, as in the garden of Eden. However, at the appointed time, God expects us to come to a greater understanding of Him so that we can discern His purpose for us.

Death is not a new thing placed on us because of Adam and Eve. Death is a part of the natural order. Without God, we go the way of the natural order. When we partake of the life of God in Jesus Christ, we will have eternal life.

Chapter Three

What Is the Gospel Message?

Now after John was put in prison, Jesus came to Galilee, preaching the gospel of the kingdom of God, and saying, "The time is fulfilled, and the kingdom of God is at hand. Repent, and believe in the gospel. (Mark 1:14-15)

When Jesus Christ began His ministry He said, "repent for the kingdom of God is at hand." Jesus Christ preached the message of the reign, or kingdom, of God. This message was called the gospel.

And this gospel of the kingdom will be preached in all the world as a witness to all the nations, and then the end will come. (Matthew 24:14)

Note, the "gospel of the kingdom" would be the gospel preached to all the world as a witness to the nations. Growing up in church, I often heard references concerning the need to preach the gospel. Our understanding of the gospel was based upon the word "gospel" which means the "good news." The question to be answered seemed simple enough. What is the good news? To us, the good news was the proclamation that Jesus Christ died for our sins and that we needed to be saved in order to go to heaven. The rejection or the lack of knowledge of this gospel would doom us to hell. The emphasis was always on the need to save souls. Our thinking was that life here on earth didn't matter much. What really counted was that we would one day go to heaven. In the end, going to heaven was all that really mattered.

According to the Scriptures, Jesus Christ went about preaching the gospel. If the message of the gospel was really the fact that Jesus Christ died on the cross for our sins, how then could Jesus have preached the gospel? How could there be a gospel if He hadn't died yet? As we begin our journey on knowing the plan and purpose of God, we need to reorient our mindsets to the message of the gospel. This message is not only the centerpiece of our proclamation but it is the center of what God has been proclaiming since the beginning of time.

Abraham is the father of the Christian faith. His faith is the example given to us to demonstrate a life that will be pleasing to God. Abraham heard the voice of God. After he heard the word, he gave action to his faith by not only believing God but by obeying the word given to him. Did you know Abraham had the gospel preached to him? The Scriptures declare Abraham heard the gospel.

> *And the Scripture, foreseeing that God would justify the Gentiles by faith, preached the gospel to Abraham beforehand, saying, "In you all the nations shall be blessed." So then those who are of faith are blessed with believing Abraham.* (Galatians 3:8-9)

What is the gospel? If Abraham heard the gospel, it must again be a message far bigger than the message of the cross since it predated the cross. The key phrase in our understanding of the gospel is "in you all nations shall be blessed." This corresponds to what Jesus Christ declared about the gospel going forth as a witness "to all nations." To understand fully God's plan and purpose, one most consider the whole counsel of the Word. This includes both the Old and the New Testament. To understand the whole context of the gospel, we need to go to the declaration of the prophet Isaiah.

How beautiful upon the mountains Are the feet of him who brings good news, Who proclaims peace, Who brings glad tidings of good things, Who proclaims salvation, Who says to Zion, "Your God reigns! (Isaiah 52:7)

The central point of the gospel, the good news, is the fact that "your God reigns." The proclamation of God's salvation and peace are components of this proclamation but not the center. Why is this adjustment in our mindsets so important? When we have the proper emphasis in our gospel message, God becomes the center in the lives of those who accept it. Since God reigns, the power of this gospel is not dependent on the response of the listener, but the power is dependent on the initiator, God! When we accept this message, we are not just accepting something from God, but we are repenting and submitting ourselves to Him. Too many people have claimed God's salvation without truly making Him their king. Jesus Christ did not come just to save the world; He came to announce the reign of God and to take His place before us as the king who sets on the throne of authority. The central message of the gospel has been lost by so many who fail to see Jesus Christ is the King of Kings and Lord of Lords, but in the end everyone will make this declaration.

Therefore God also has highly exalted Him and given Him the name which is above every name, that at the name of Jesus every knee should bow, of those in heaven, and of those on earth, and of those under the earth, and that every tongue should confess that Jesus Christ is Lord, to the glory of God the Father. (Philippians 2:9-11)

We are living in a day when many people are following a man centered gospel. Many people come to church looking for what is in it for them. I believe and have always preached that, "we should bless the Lord and forget not all of His benefits." The psalmist declared this, and I have certainly come to experience the many benefits of serving the awesome God. To me, God's great salvation covers every area of my life. However, His salvation is not the center of my life, His "Lordship" is. To bless the Lord, is not just to sing a good praise song and then be inspired with words telling you what God wants to do for you. The word bless means to "bow down" or "to prostrate oneself" before another. We need to learn how to truly bless the Lord. We need to truly understand what worship is.

> *Oh come, let us worship and bow down; Let us kneel before the LORD our Maker. For He is our God, And we are the people of His pasture, And the sheep of His hand. Today, if you will hear His voice:* (Psalm 95:6-7)

It was a lack of understanding the gospel that hindered the children of Israel from entering the Promised Land. Of course, most people have never noticed the gospel was preached to the children of Israel. Yes, the gospel was preached to them; but for them, unlike their father, Abraham, they did not walk in faith.

> *Therefore, since a promise remains of entering His rest, let us fear lest any of you seem to have come short of it. For indeed the gospel was preached to us as well as to them; but the word which they heard did not profit them, not being mixed with faith in those who heard it. For we who have believed do enter that rest, as He has said: "So I swore in My wrath, 'They shall not enter My rest,'" although the works were finished from the foundation of the world.* (Hebrews 4:1-3)

The children of Israel were walking in God's salvation. As a people, they had been in the bondage of Egypt for 400 years. God raised up Moses to deliver them. They experienced God's salvation with an almighty hand through many miraculous works. After they left Egypt, they met the Lord at Mount Sinai and had a great encounter with the power of the living God. The mountain of the Lord shook with His power, and the cloud of His presence sat upon the mountain. This same presence led them through the wilderness giving them direction and a covering from the torturous desert heat.

When they needed food or water, God gave them a miraculous provision. Yet, when they arrived at the waters of the Promised Land, they refused to go into the land. What was the problem? There were giants in the land. The promise was everything God had said it would be, but the giants were an unexpected development. When the children of Israel saw the giants, the Bible says they "saw themselves as grasshoppers before them." They had lost sight of the gospel, and so they lost sight of God. They lost sight of the fact that "their God reigns."

When the children of Israel refused to go in to possess the Promised Land, the Lord became very angry. God said to Moses, "How long will this people reject me?" (When you reject God's promises, you really are rejecting God.) God took this rejection personally. Why? Because when we reject God's purpose, we are rejecting Him for who He is. God is the almighty God. When He calls us, He calls us to His purpose. How could He not take it personally? God was ready to send pestilence upon them and disinherit them. Moses cried out for God's mercy for His people. God consented to show mercy, but He did so with a stipulation.

> *Then the LORD said: "I have pardoned, according to your word; but truly, as I live, all the earth shall be filled with the glory of the LORD — because all these men who have seen My glory and the signs which I did in Egypt and in the wilderness, and have put Me to the test now these ten times, and have not heeded My voice, they certainly shall not see the land of which I swore to their fathers, nor shall any of those who rejected Me see it.* (Numbers 14:20-23)

Our response to God does not deter God from His purpose. He declares in the midst of the failure of His people His intent to fulfill His purpose. Like in the garden of Eden when Adam and Eve sinned, God still proclaims His eternal purpose will be fulfilled. One day there will be people willing to believe God. Currently, there are people wanting God's mercy but not wanting to extend themselves in faith to believe they can be everything God wants them to be.

This is a common response in our day. People want God's grace to pardon them of their weakness but do not want His grace to empower them to fulfill His purpose. What kind of person are you?

The issue was not what the people of God could do but what their God could do. If you don't see God for who He is, you will see yourself or you will see your enemy. Neither of these perspectives will enable you to take the land God says He wants to give you. This is why we need to have a proper perspective of the gospel. If you have a gospel that says "God reigns," you will never become focused on yourself or your enemy. Your focus will be on God. This is a day when God wants to raise up His people as a mighty witness to the nations. The Scriptures declare, *"in the latter days that the mountain of the Lord's house shall be established on the top of the mountains, and shall be exalted above the hills."* It goes on to say, *"And all nations shall flow to it."* The gospel of the kingdom preached by Jesus Christ and also preached to our father, Abraham, is a gospel to the nations. It is a declaration of the reign of God in the earth. It is not a declaration of what can be but what is already a reality. A reality not seen and confessed but a reality that is very real. The reality of the kingdom of God must be preached and believed until the reality of its full manifestation. It will happen!

Had the children of Israel walked in this reality they would have never doubted the promise of God. They would have seen the land flowing with milk and honey, and they would have known it was theirs for the taking. Because they did not believe the gospel of the reign of God, they lost hold of their possession. They also lost something more valuable than their inheritance. They lost out on the rest God gives to His people. There came a day when the children of Israel took possession of the land of promise, but even then they missed the greater blessing. It is this blessing God wants to give to us in this great day of visitation.

> *Since therefore it remains that some must enter it, and those to whom it was first preached did not enter because of disobedience, again He designates a certain day, saying in David, "Today," after such a long time, as it has been said:*

"Today, if you will hear His voice, Do not harden your hearts." For if Joshua had given them rest, then He would not afterward have spoken of another day. There remains therefore a rest for the people of God. (Hebrews 4:6-9)

After the children of Israel took possession of the land, they demonstrated what happens when we fail to enter into the rest of God. Remember the importance of the Sabbath. They not only failed to fully serve the Lord but they also never walked in the satisfied life God wanted them to experience. The end result was that they eventually lost the land of their inheritance and missed out on the blessing God had for them. To experience God's blessing, you have to be a person who blesses God. How do we bless God? We bless God by kneeling before Him and acknowledging His sovereignty in the world and in our lives. God is not a tool we use to gain control of our world, but we become a tool or vessel God can use to rule in His world. When we bless the Lord, the blessing of His kingdom will be fully experienced by us.

The Scriptures declare, *"today, if you will hear His voice."* I believe this is a new day for the people of God. This is a day when God wants to speak to us and give us the faith to fully possess the land of our inheritance. This level of faith can only come if we hear and respond to the message of the gospel declared by Jesus Christ. A gospel that so inspired our father, Abraham, he was willing to give up everything he had and knew to follow after what God had for him. Not only would he be blessed but everyone who blessed him would be blessed, and those who cursed him would be cursed. The Word stated that Abraham would be a blessing. His seed would be a blessing in every nation of the earth. It is time for us to walk fully in the blessings of Abraham, our father!

Abraham received the promise of God that said he would make his name great. Now, thousands of years later, you and I can see the faithfulness of God and the power of the walk of faith. Through religious persuasion or natural ancestry, literally billions of people consider Abraham to be their father. Isn't God's word amazing? It is time for the seed of Abraham, by faith, to rise up in

49

the earth and be the source of blessing God has called us to be. The world needs us. Our countries need us. Our families need us. Will you open yourself up to a new level of faith, so you can go beyond the "bless me" stage to the place where God will pour you out a blessing to the world around you?

With this in mind, can you comprehend how important our understanding of the gospel message is? Anything short of the gospel of the kingdom of God will cause us to miss the message Jesus Christ Himself wanted to communicate to us. When Jesus Christ hung on the cross He declared, *"It is finished."*

> *So when Jesus had received the sour wine, He said, "It is fin-*
> *ished!" And bowing His head, He gave up His spirit.* (John
> 19:30)

I have often heard people talk about the finished work of the cross. To them, everything either points to the cross, as is the case of the Old Testament, or points back to the cross in relationship to the New Testament and its impact on us today. Certainly, we must see the importance of the cross, but we must also understand the cross is another of the ongoing steps God has pre-ordained leading to the fullness of His plan from the beginning. When God ceased from His labors because He had finished the work, it was not only about the cross. The cross represents to us the twofold aspect of God's plan leading to the fulfillment of His purpose. (God begins as the Creator then follows up His plan as the Savior.) The God who creates also saves.

> *For thus says the LORD, Who created the heavens, Who is*
> *God, Who formed the earth and made it, Who has estab-*
> *lished it, Who did not create it in vain, Who formed it to be*
> *inhabited: Tell and bring forth your case; Yes, let them take*
> *counsel together. Who has declared this from ancient time?*
> *Who has told it from that time? Have not I, the LORD? And*
> *there is no other God besides Me, A just God and a Savior;*
> *There is none besides Me. "Look to Me, and be saved, All you*

ends of the earth! For I am God, and there is no other. (Isaiah 45:18, 21-22)

God did not create the earth in vain! He did not create it as something worthless or without purpose. He created it with a purpose and as a place to be inhabited. This word "inhabited" means a place to be settled or to dwell in. This is what the announcement of the kingdom of God by Jesus Christ was all about. It was to announce the plan and purpose God has had from the beginning for planet Earth and for the people of the earth. This is why the prayer of the kingdom, commonly called the "Lord's Prayer" or the "Our Father," encourages us to pray for the will of God to be done in the earth as it is in heaven. God wants to bring heaven to earth. God wants the earth to be a place of His habitation. This habitation will be His resting place. This resting place is not just the earth but His people who are on the earth.

> *For the LORD has chosen Zion; He has desired it for His dwelling place: "This is My resting place forever; Here I will dwell, for I have desired it. I will abundantly bless her provision; I will satisfy her poor with bread.* (Psalm 132:13-15)

When God has His resting place, it will be a place of great blessing for His people. Great blessings flow from the abiding presence of the Almighty. But God's abiding place needs to be a resting place. We must become the people of rest God has called us to be. From the resting place we have prepared for God, He will send the rod of His strength.

> *The LORD said to my Lord, "Sit at My right hand, Till I make Your enemies Your footstool." The LORD shall send the rod of Your strength out of Zion. Rule in the midst of Your enemies!* (Psalm 110:1-2)

Note, He will rule in the midst of His enemies. Since the time of man's disobedience in the garden, there has been an opposition to the rule of God. In order to be a people of rest, we must understand this opposition exists by permission from God. God and His kingdom are never under threat from the forces of opposition. These forces exist to be used as a tool of God for His purpose. The book of the Revelation talks about Babylon, the city of harlots. This is in opposition to the city of God. God's city is seen as a chaste bride. Babylon is a whore who lives off the pleasures of the world. Babylon is the world outside the Holy City or the kingdom of God. To understand how God uses the opposing city, we need to go to the story of the children of Israel in the time they came under the rule of Babylon.

Babylon was a rising power that was a threat to all the nations around her. God had promised His protection over His people as long as they were obedient to follow His voice. Unfortunately, they rebelled against God, so God sent the message by the voice of His prophets about an impending judgment. The house of Israel did not want to believe these prophets, so God allowed them to hear what they wanted to hear from a multitude of false prophets. Remember, God not only gives us a choice but He will give us an advocate to convince us it is okay to do what we want to do. It was that way in the garden, and it will always be that way until the end. The false prophets said God would never allow the Holy City to come under judgment. Their protection was in their place as the people of God living in the presence of God. Surely God would not allow the Holy City and the holy people to be desecrated. It is this false notion that has caused many people in history to resist God and count on the glory of the past to protect them. How many moves of God are only remnants of their former glory? God not only sent Babylon to destroy the Holy City and the temple but He would use this occasion to deliver His people.

> *Be in pain, and labor to bring forth, O daughter of Zion, Like a woman in birth pangs. For now you shall go forth from the city, You shall dwell in the field, And to Babylon you shall go. There you shall be delivered; There the LORD will redeem you From the hand of your enemies.* (Micah 4:10)

In Babylon, God would deal with His people and would provide a powerful witness to Babylon about the superiority of God's ways. Many of us know the story of Daniel and his companions whose fierce stand for God brought a great testimony to Babylon. One day King Nebuchadnezzar had a dream. In the vision of his dream, he saw a great tree whose branches reached the nations of the earth. The birds landed on the tree, the beasts of the field huddled under its shade, and the fruit of the tree with its abundance provided food for everyone. The tree was cut down to a stump with its roots left in the ground. He then heard a voice speaking concerning the tree that changed and appeared to be talking more about a person. The voice said to let his heart be changed from the heart of a person to the heart of an animal and let seven times pass over him. None of the wise men of Babylon could give the suitable interpretation of the dream, so the king called for Daniel whom he knew had a relationship with the "Holy" God. The word "holy" means one set apart. The king knew there was something different about the God of Daniel because of the great power His servants demonstrated. There was something different about Daniel too. Daniel had been set apart by God.

The interpretation of the dream was not a good one for the king. He would have his kingdom taken from him and for a period of time would be a madman. But so that he would know the Most High rules in the kingdom of men, his kingdom would be given back to him. It would have been a very unusual thing for a king to lose his kingdom and then have it given back to him. In those days, someone was always sitting on the sidelines waiting to take advantage of any situation. Family members were not exempt from the tyranny of those days. Killing relatives to secure the throne was very customary. The added part here was the mental affliction that would besiege the king. He would become like an animal, so all the customary attitudes of respect for the sovereign would have been discarded. The only way this could happen is by some divine intervention. As long as we can trust in our own power or the hand of man, we rarely recognize God is at work. God was going to make His power evident to a heathen king.

After his trial, the king makes a mighty declaration of the lesson he had learned.

> *And at the end of the time I, Nebuchadnezzar, lifted my eyes to heaven, and my understanding returned to me; and I blessed the Most High and praised and honored Him who lives forever: For His dominion is an everlasting dominion, And His kingdom is from generation to generation. All the inhabitants of the earth are reputed as nothing; He does according to His will in the army of heaven And among the inhabitants of the earth. No one can restrain His hand Or say to Him, "What have You done?" (Daniel 4:34-35)*

This lesson of the Bible is a very important lesson about God. It is a testimony that is just as true today as it ever was. It was an especially revolutionary concept in the times of Nebuchadnezzar. Most every country or city-state had their own god. Some had several gods, but usually they saw one as the prominent one. To them, gods were like people always competing with each other and with man. When the Babylonians captured the Jews, they would have seen this as a sign of the power of their god over the God of Israel. They would likely have accepted the existence of this God but would surely have made every effort to convince the Jews of the superiority of their god. This is why they tried to force the Jews to worship their god for it would have been a sign of their submission to them.

The Jews themselves would have been conflicted about these events. Because the false prophets had told them they would never come under judgment, how could God allow this to happen and still maintain His claim of being the Almighty revealed to Abraham? They didn't understand that when you know who you are, you don't have to prove yourself to anybody. God is motivated by His plan and purpose not His need for approval as we so often are. God is not insecure about who He is, so He doesn't have to prove Himself to anybody. He is faithful to His Word.

Now, through the use of his spiritual insight, Daniel would be able to interpret the king's dream and show the superiority of God's insight over the insight of man. Nebuchadnezzar had many advisors who used the wisdom of the time. He had sorceries, divinations, and magic which seems like simple superstition to the modern mind but was considered the prevailing knowledge of the time. Many modern people fail to admit the origin of modern medicine comes from the witch doctors of yesterday who used their potions for helping the people. Our research and development of these potions has improved, but the roots are still the same. I do not say this to discredit modern science but to place it in the appropriate historical setting. Babylon had the best wisdom of their time, but it couldn't stand against the wisdom of God. Modern alternatives, although giving great help to man, still cannot substitute for the wisdom of God. We are living in a modern era when man believes He has solutions for everything apart from God. The same God who demonstrated His glory in the days of Daniel will do so again in our day. We, in the kingdom of God, armed with the Word, need to demonstrate our confidence in God. As the expert advice of the world becomes more apparently futile, the wisdom of God's Word will become more recognized as the source of true knowledge and wisdom.

In Babylon, God established the fact that He was not just the God of Israel but the God of the whole earth. The Lord God is the Lord "Most" High. He established the fact that He rules in the affairs of heaven but also in the affairs of men. This is certainly not a localized or limited power. The God of Israel led His people into captivity in Babylon and made known He ruled there as well as in Israel. The temple and the Holy City had a special place in God's domain, but it was not the limit of His domain. The Scriptures tell us the people of God form the center of God's concern and are the center of His work. When God declared the house of Israel as His special treasure, it meant everything revolved around them.

When the Most High divided their inheritance to the nations,
When He separated the sons of Adam, He set the boundaries

> *of the peoples According to the number of the children of Is-*
> *rael. For the LORD's portion is His people; Jacob is the place*
> *of His inheritance.* (Deuteronomy 32:8-9)

There is an important paradigm we need in the church today. When Jesus Christ came to the earth, He announced the kingdom of God was at hand. Jesus also told the people how they could see and enter the kingdom of God through the process of the new birth. As Christians, we are supposed to seek first the kingdom of God and know that when we do this all the other things of life we desire will be added to us. From this perspective, we often get the mindset held by the house of Israel before the judgment through Babylon came upon them. We seemingly limit God to the realm of His special treasure or people. I have often heard the description of the kingdom as the realm under the sovereign reign of a king. In other words, the kingdom extends to the limits of those submitted to the king. This is often the thought process of the Christian even though we sometimes do not think it is. We will say that God is Lord of everything, but in practice we actually limit His power. This is why we often think the world is out of control and on a crash course of judgment. We see the kingdom as God's domain left under the power of satan who often rises up as a threat to us. When you watch world news, do you know God rules over all things? When you are at work interacting with the world, do you realize God is in control of your work place? Yes, He allows a certain level of freedom of choice; but when it comes to His people and His purpose, you must understand God always holds the power! When you know that, you do a lot more praying than you do worrying.

This is why the Father can give us the kingdom. Everything is ultimately in God's hands to use at His discretion. When the people of God are faithful in their stewardship, God is able to reward them with the things not in their hands. Even if it is the wilderness, or Babylon, it is still in God's hands to give. This is why God could use Babylon as His tool of judgment then turn around and punish them for what they had done to His people. Whatever we see that seems to be in the hands of any person or people, we must understand it still belongs to God when in His discretion He decides to use it. This is why He could dispossess the people of the land of Canaan to give the land to His people, Israel, and why He could in turn dispossess them when they were unfaithful to Him. We must remember God is the possessor of heaven and earth and everything is His to give.

> *And he blessed him and said: "Blessed be Abram of God Most High, Possessor of heaven and earth; And blessed be God Most High, Who has delivered your enemies into your hand." And he gave him a tithe of all.* (Genesis 14:19-20)

In Summary

It is essential for us to understand both the need to proclaim the gospel and what the gospel message actually is. The gospel is the "good news," but what is the good news? The central point of the gospel or the good news is the fact that "your God reigns." When we speak of the gospel we typically talk about the message of salvation. The proclamation of God's salvation and peace are components of the gospel message but not the center. Why is this adjustment in our mindsets so important? When we have the proper emphasis in our gospel message, God becomes the center in the lives of those who accept it. Since God reigns, the power of this gospel is not dependent on the response of the listener, but the power is dependent on the initiator, God. We cannot stop at accepting God's salvation. We must make Him the King and Lord of our life.

Our walk with God is not about us; it is about Him and His purpose. Our response to God does not deter Him from His purpose. People want God's grace to pardon them of their weakness but do not want His grace to empower them to fulfill His purpose. The issue is not what the people of God can do but what God can do. If you have a gospel that says "God reigns," you will never become focused on yourself or your enemy. Your focus will be on God.

When you recognize that "your God reigns," you can possess all that God has for you including the rest that God has for His people.

We must learn to bless the Lord by kneeling before Him and acknowledging His sovereignty in the world and in our lives. God is not a tool we use to gain control of our world, but we become a tool or vessel God can use to rule in His world. When we bless the Lord, the blessing of His kingdom will be fully experienced by us.

God rules in the whole earth. It is important that we see the knowledge and wisdom of God as the true source of all knowledge and wisdom. God's reign has no limits. He has power in heaven and on earth. As Christians, we seek first the kingdom of God and all the other things of life we desire will be added unto us. We must understand that God always holds the power. Everything is ultimately in His hands. God is the possessor of heaven and earth and everything is His to give.

Chapter Four

Do You Know You Were Designed for an Eternal Purpose?

By faith he dwelt in the land of promise as in a foreign coun-
try, dwelling in tents with Isaac and Jacob, the heirs with him
of the same promise; for he waited for the city which has foun-
dations, whose builder and maker is God. (Hebrews 11:9-10)

Abraham was the father of our faith. We, who believe God and
make a choice to follow God, are of the seed of faith. The Word
declares that Abraham, *"waited for the city which has foundations,*
whose builder and maker is God." (The place of rest God desires to
take us is a place where we are looking for what God is building not
what we are building. God's kingdom is not a man made system; it
is something God has built.)The Promised Land is a place God has
prepared for us. In the Old Testament God had His people build a
replica of the heavenly realm. This was to show them God's pattern
but also to show them the work God was going to do.

But Christ came as High Priest of the good things to come,
with the greater and more perfect tabernacle not made with
hands, that is, not of this creation. (Hebrews 9:11)

The words we started this chapter with in Hebrews 11:10:
"builder and maker" literally mean designer-builder. This concept is
very important in our consideration of what God is doing in history and what He is doing in our individual lives. The first look at
the person of God, reveals Him as the creator of the heavens, the
earth, and all things pertaining to them. As God creates the crown-

ing glory of His creation, man, we see God is also a God who has established a purpose in all He has created. I want us to look at this purpose, how it has unfolded before us, and how it will continue to unfold in the future.

In the early days of the church that I pastor, as we were preparing for the future of our ministry, we had to make plans for a new building. We were sold on a concept called design/build. This concept meant the company building the building would also be the designer. This would help us understand the cost effective ways we could employ in our project, so we could have the most efficient use of our resources, since the designer and builder were one. The designer/builder was able to give us all the knowledge ahead of time, so we could anticipate and resolve the problems we would face with every design and choice we made for our building. When the construction began, the builder couldn't blame the designer, and the designer couldn't pass the buck to the builder because they were the same person.

When going back to the creation, we must see God's purpose is being served through a design/build process. The creation was the beginning of the purpose of God in the earth. Remember what Abraham has taught us. The things God builds also have a foundation that come from God. When I look at the unfolding of God's plan and purpose in the earth, I always have this in mind. What God is building always has a foundation. The Scriptures declare God is a God who builds line upon line and precept, or principle, upon precept. He builds a little here and a little there. God is never in a hurry because His desire is to do things right, not do it fast. This part of the character of God leads to a lot of frustration for the people of God who are much less patient than God. The key to a good building will be in the proper foundation. In the beginning, God laid the foundation for His purpose and has been unfolding it ever since. Having a foundation, means God is not building in a random fashion, neither is He always changing what He is doing. When God is involved, we should be able to see the ongoing development with a beginning and a consummated end. This represents the character of God when we see Him as the Alpha and Omega, the Beginning and the End.

> *And behold, I am coming quickly, and My reward is with Me, to give to every one according to his work. I am the Alpha and the Omega, the Beginning and the End, the First and the Last.* (Revelation 22:12-13)

When the culmination of history is fulfilled, we will understand God has been at work throughout the ages: past, present, and future. I believe we must see the lack of this understanding to be the source of a lot of the difficulties people have in relating to God's plan and purpose. So, faith says not only is God a designer, His design existed before time began.

> *Indeed My hand has laid the foundation of the earth, And My right hand has stretched out the heavens; When I call to them, They stand up together.* (Isaiah 48:13)

Believing the work of God has foundations, we must be very careful that we have confidence in what God has started. Often, as we are moving forward in the things of God, we look back questioning how we can reconcile the past with the present and future.

When we started the construction of the present location of our main church ministry, we had some problems when we were laying the foundation. Because the property has a high water table and a wetland consistency in the soil, extra care had to be given to the foundation construction. The inspector was right on sight to watch and make sure we were laying a good foundation. In the beginning, it was raining, making the soil even more porous. The inspector insisted we keep adding metal with the cement. I didn't see metal. As the metal was added, I saw dollar signs as we were required to add more and more to our foundation. Regardless of the cost, the truth is that after the construction of the building no one thinks about foundations unless you have a problem. I am sure our building has a good foundation because I was there. I saw the cost.

I wasn't there when God laid the foundations of the earth, but because I know Him I have confidence in His work. The master designer/builder will surely have a good foundation under what He is building, so I don't need to look back. I can always look confidently to the future. When God laid the foundation of the earth, He was able to do it without our advice.

> *Who has directed the Spirit of the LORD, Or as His counselor has taught Him? Have you not known? Have you not heard? Has it not been told you from the beginning? Have you not understood from the foundations of the earth? It is He who sits above the circle of the earth, And its inhabitants are like grasshoppers, Who stretches out the heavens like a curtain, And spreads them out like a tent to dwell in.* (Isaiah 40:13, 21-22)

As individual Christians, we must also see this principle in our own lives. Many people see the work of God beginning in their lives at the time of conversion or sometimes in the situations leading up to their conversion. This is not what Jesus Christ taught. He made it clear the foundation of our conversion and call began long before our choice. Most importantly, He says we could not even come to the Lord if it were not for the active work of the Father in our life before we came to Him.

> *No one can come to Me unless the Father who sent Me draws him; and I will raise him up at the last day. It is written in the prophets, 'And they shall all be taught by God.' Therefore everyone who has heard and learned from the Father comes to Me.* (John 6:44-45)

(The foundation of your walk with God was not when you responded, but when God chose you to be a part.) When did God choose you? God chose you before the foundation of the earth.

> *just as He chose us in Him before the foundation of the world, that we should be holy and without blame before Him*

in love, having predestined us to adoption as sons by Jesus Christ to Himself, according to the good pleasure of His will, to the praise of the glory of His grace, by which He made us accepted in the Beloved. (Ephesians 1:4-6)

Now to go to our foundation, we have to take a step even further back. Not only did He choose you(He also created you with a specific purpose in mind.)God was involved in your genetics and took an active part in your forming in the womb for His purpose in the earth.

For You formed my inward parts; You covered me in my mother's womb. I will praise You, for I am fearfully and wonderfully made; Marvelous are Your works, And that my soul knows very well. My frame was not hidden from You, When I was made in secret, And skillfully wrought in the lowest parts of the earth. Your eyes saw my substance, being yet unformed. And in Your book they all were written, The days fashioned for me, When as yet there were none of them. How precious also are Your thoughts to me, O God! How great is the sum of them! (Psalm 139:13-17)

How awesome is that? Talk about the foundations of what God builds! God not only chose you but you were intricately and wonderfully made and designed for the eternal purpose of God. Every good designer will be sure that they know the qualities of the component parts of their project. Not only were you chosen to be a part of the plan and purpose of God but you are "the" part. You were chosen, yes, but you also were(designed for the purpose of God.) Just think, God not only designs the building but He designs every component part He has chosen for His building. You must see your significant qualities as having been bestowed by the master designer to be used for His purpose in the earth.

Woe to him who strives with his Maker! Let the potsherd strive with the potsherds of the earth! Shall the clay say to him who forms it, 'What are you making?' Or shall your handiwork say, 'He has no hands'? Woe to him who says to his father, 'What are you begetting?' Or to the woman, 'What have you brought forth?'" Thus says the LORD, The Holy One of Israel, and his Maker:" Ask Me of things to come concerning My sons; And concerning the work of My hands, you command Me. (Isaiah 45:9-11)

This admonition from the prophet Isaiah was not intended to be seen only as a principle applying to the individual but also to mankind.

I have made the earth, And created man on it. I — My hands — stretched out the heavens, And all their host I have commanded. I have raised him up in righteousness, And I will direct all his ways; He shall build My city And let My exiles go free, Not for price nor reward," says the LORD of hosts. (Isaiah 45:12-13)

Mankind was created for a specific purpose. From the viewpoint of many people, we are so flawed we are "depraved" and without the ability to fulfill the purpose of God. How can we say this about a creature God Himself created "in His own image and likeness"? In our natural state, we are certainly in need of God's power to raise us up in righteousness, but we must see God's plan from the beginning and understand it is without mistakes or malfunction. God's plan needs the guiding hand He so willingly has offered; but with His salvation from our natural state, we should certainly see the prize possession the Lord has claimed as His own. God did not create us depraved but simply a people who find their completeness in God's great salvation.

Tell and bring forth your case; Yes, let them take counsel together. Who has declared this from ancient time? Who has told it from that time? Have not I, the LORD? And there is no other God besides Me, A just God and a Savior; There is none besides Me. "Look to Me, and be saved, All you ends of the earth! For I am God, and there is no other. (Isaiah 45:21-22)

You were created to be the source in which God would reach the world. His ultimate plan was not just that He would use us for His purpose but that we would be the channel He would use in giving the world access to Him.

> *Thus says the LORD: "The labor of Egypt and merchandise of Cush And of the Sabeans, men of stature, Shall come over to you, and they shall be yours; They shall walk behind you, They shall come over in chains; And they shall bow down to you. They will make supplication to you, saying, 'Surely God is in you, And there is no other; There is no other God.'"* (Isaiah 45:14)

We generally think God can have no real use for us. When we survey the human condition from our own eyes, we have a tendency to believe God is going to somehow have to push us aside. How could God really fulfill His purpose through man? No wonder the prophet went on to say that God really knows how to hide Himself when He chose to live in us.

> *Truly You are God, who hide Yourself, O God of Israel, the Savior!* (Isaiah 45:15)

God desires us to believe He did this, and then to understand He wants us to do the same.

Many Christians confess they walk in faith but really have little confidence in God's design ability. If God is a designer, we must be careful not to think that the plan of God is being hindered or altered based upon our human response. If God is the designer the Word declares him to be, surely, He would have factored in our response as part of the plan. When I examine the Word of God, I certainly can see the truth in this. Since God has designed us for His purpose, we know His salvation includes His ability to coordinate His plans with our actions. From this perspective, we see everything contributes to His purpose.

And we know that all things work together for good to those who love God, to those who are the called according to His purpose. For whom He foreknew, He also predestined to be conformed to the image of His Son, that He might be the firstborn among many brethren. Moreover whom He predestined, these He also called; whom He called, these He also justified; and whom He justified, these He also glorified. What then shall we say to these things? If God is for us, who can be against us? (Romans 8:28-31)

Can you believe "all things" work together for the good? If it is in fact all things, that means even when you get in the way, God still has the perfect plan. He will factor our response into His purpose. God may not be the cause of all things, but He can use all things. As a builder, He can take what we give to Him and use it for His purpose. Both we and our actions are a part of this design/builder inventory. How does God do this? In His mercy, He redeems our lives from destruction. God's redemptive plan is to take our actions and turn them into a good purpose.

Who redeems your life from destruction, Who crowns you with lovingkindness and tender mercies, (Psalm 103:4)

The life of Joseph is such a great example of this. I know when we read about the way his brothers treated him, we see selling him into slavery as just an evil action. But if you look closely at the story, you will note that his father unfairly treated him by favoring him over his brothers. He took advantage of this by telling on his brothers when they did wrong, no doubt, to make himself look better. No wonder his brothers hated him. So when he was sold into slavery, it wasn't just their actions God had to redeem but Joseph's also. I would imagine this impacted Joseph's actions at the time his brothers came to him in Egypt. His mercy to them, no doubt, was given as a result of seeing the mercy of God in his own life. At every step of the way, God, our Father, is teaching and instructing us, and we need to be sensitive to God and the people God uses in our life.

This is why I have such confidence in the church. When I began in the ministry at age twenty-four, I started a church. As I was inquiring of God about what to call the church, He not only gave me the name of the church but a vision for our church based upon His plan for the church as a whole as recorded in Isaiah 2.

> *Now it shall come to pass in the latter days That the mountain of the LORD's house Shall be established on the top of the mountains, And shall be exalted above the hills; And all nations shall flow to it. Many people shall come and say, "Come, and let us go up to the mountain of the LORD, To the house of the God of Jacob; He will teach us His ways, And we shall walk in His paths." For out of Zion shall go forth the law, And the word of the LORD from Jerusalem.* (Isaiah 2:2-3)

As I mentioned earlier, I do believe God's eternal purpose is for a glorious and victorious church. I also believe this because I have great confidence in God as a builder. Jesus made a declaration of this fact to the apostles. One day He questioned them as to who people were saying He was. After hearing what they had heard, He asked them the pointed question: "Who do you say that I am?" Each and every one of us must have faith born from a personal conviction not just what we hear other people saying. When Peter affirmed His belief that Jesus Christ was indeed the Son of the living God, Jesus made a strong declaration of His intent.

> *Jesus answered and said to him, "Blessed are you, Simon Bar-Jonah, for flesh and blood has not revealed this to you, but My Father who is in heaven. And I also say to you that you are Peter, and on this rock I will build My church, and the gates of Hades shall not prevail against it. And I will give you the keys of the kingdom of heaven, and whatever you bind on earth will be bound in heaven, and whatever you loose on earth will be loosed in heaven."* (Matthew 16:17-19)

What was the revelation that made Peter very blessed? It was the revelation of who Jesus Christ was. With this revelation, you will have confidence in everything He says. When Jesus Christ says, *"I will build my church"* and *"The gates of hades shall not prevail against it,"* you should have every confidence it will come to pass. Don't look at yourself or other people; but look to Him, and you will have the confidence to see His salvation power to the nations! From my personal relationship with Jesus Christ, I have learned to have confidence in His Word. If He says it, it must be true, no matter how impossible it might seem to us. The things that are impossible for man are possible when God is involved. When God is building something, the gates of hell will not prevail; but the Word of God will prevail. Don't be limited in your faith based upon human ability, but put your trust in the living God.

> *But Jesus looked at them and said, "With men it is impossible, but not with God; for with God all things are possible."* (Mark 10:27)

Abraham, the father, grew in faith as he grew in the knowledge of who God was. His revelation of the person of God grew and was manifested according to the situations he would face. Your faith will not grow because you have tried to develop your faith. Your faith will grow as you grow in your relationship with God. We are living in an important time in history. God is calling His church to arise and fulfill His purpose in the earth. To take a step higher in faith, we need to see God in a clearer light. When God came to Abraham to encourage him to go further, He also made an announcement about Himself.

> *When Abram was ninety-nine years old, the LORD appeared to Abram and said to him, "I am Almighty God; walk before Me and be blameless. And I will make My covenant between Me and you, and will multiply you exceedingly.* (Genesis 17:1-2)

As you approach the reading of this book, ask the Lord to open your eyes to see Him as the true design/builder, and let yourself see a fresh perspective of what He is doing in the earth and in your life!

In Summary

God's kingdom is not a man made system; it is something God has built. He is the designer. He is also the builder. God starts with a foundation and then adds line upon line. God is not building in a random fashion; He is building according to His plan. The foundation of your conversion and call began long before your choice to accept Him. The foundation of your walk with God began when God chose you to be a part of His plan. Not only did God choose you, He also created you with a specific purpose in mind. God was involved in your genetics and took an active part in your forming in the womb for His purpose in the earth. He designed you! God did not create you depraved but simply a people who find their completeness in God's great salvation.

His ultimate plan was not just that He would use us for His purpose but that we would be the channel He would use in giving the world access to Him. Since God has designed us for His purpose, we know His salvation includes His ability to coordinate His plans with our actions. From this perspective, we see everything contributes to His purpose. We must be careful not to think that the plan of God is being hindered or altered based upon our human response. Even when we get in the way, God still has the perfect plan. He will factor our response into His purpose. God may not be the cause of all things, but He can use all things. As a builder, He can take what we give to Him and use it for His purpose. In His mercy, He redeems our lives from destruction.

When God says something it will come to pass no matter how impossible it seems. We must have confidence in His Word.

Don't be limited in your faith based upon human ability, but put your trust in the living God. Your faith will not grow because you have tried to develop your faith. Your faith will grow as you grow in your relationship with God.

Chapter Five

How Does God Use the "What You Do" to Become the "Who You Are"?

The voice said, "Cry out!" And he said, "What shall I cry?"
"All flesh is grass, And all its loveliness is like the flower of the
field. The grass withers, the flower fades, Because the breath
of the LORD blows upon it; Surely the people are grass. The
grass withers, the flower fades, But the word of our God
stands forever. (Isaiah 40:6-8)

Due to the fact that the plan of God is revealed over time, we often think the plan is changing. As a result of being man centered rather than God centered in our thinking, we also have a tendency to think the plan must be altered to meet our response to the plan. We must understand this is not the case. As God Almighty, with an eternal plan, we must understand how God stands above and over the human condition. God has already declared it; all flesh is grass. The issue then is not the power of human flesh but the power of God's Word to perform His intent. Our efforts will last for a while, but God's purpose will endure forever. We must not be swayed from our faith because of the failure of man. It is expected and factored in. God is the almighty God, and His plan will not be altered by our response. Since God is the almighty God, there is no purpose of His that can or will be withheld from Him.

Then Job answered the LORD and said: "I know that you can
do everything, And that no purpose of yours can be withheld
from you. (Job 42:1-2)

71

Job went through a great time of testing before he came to this conclusion. In the time of his testing, everyone wanted to blame him for his circumstance. Unfortunately, since the garden of Eden, we have tried to point the finger of blame. We blame each other or we blame the devil for our problems; but in the end, we must recognize God is the Almighty, and His purpose will always come to pass. The question is: <u>Will we willingly submit ourselves to the sovereign God or will we seek to go our own way</u>? God has obviously factored human response into His plan, but I do not see anywhere that He has said our choices have altered it. Since God is Alpha and Omega, the Beginning and the End, we must assume through His foreknowledge He knew of our choices. It makes sense to assume God's plan is gradual in order to give us the time necessary to conform to His plan and to recover from our failures as we respond to His plan. This should give us hope for ourselves individually when we make mistakes, but it should also fill us with love and admiration for a God who loves us so much He has made a great effort to allow us to be a part of His plan.

Of course, the key factor in our understanding is our comprehension of God's original intent for us. He has chosen us in love to be His sons. This means Christianity is no mere religion. The Scriptures tell us the sons of God were first called Christians in the city of Antioch. This term stuck, but it was not God's choice for us. Although we are certainly followers of Jesus Christ, which is what the term Christian means, the term gave the world an opportunity to classify us as a religious group when we are far more than that. We are the sons of God in the earth, and by this we are also the family of God. God is our Father. By following Christ, we can become the children of God, making Him the firstborn of many brethren as the Scriptures declare.

Just think how much more complicated it would be for the world to conform us to their patterns if we resisted their effort to make us just another religion. We are not a religious group but the family of God. With this frame of thinking, we will also look at ourselves and God from a whole different perspective. From this perspective, we can see God as a loving and caring Father who has been nurturing and training mankind for His eternal purpose for them. Like the firstborn Son, Jesus Christ, we were born to bring glory and honor to God through our obedience and by conforming to His plan for our life. Like the firstborn Son, our life from our nativity has had meaning and purpose. All things have been working toward the goal of God being manifested and glorified through us.

> *And we know that all things work together for good to those who love God, to those who are the called according to His purpose.* (Romans 8:28)

The prophet Isaiah spoke of the early childhood of Jesus in Isaiah 53: "He grew up before the Father as a tender plant, a root out of the dry ground. He had no beauty that we would desire Him, He was a man of sorrows acquainted with grief." All of this was necessary for His earthly ministry. He wasn't just born a man of compassion; but His compassion, the ability to feel the pain of others, was given to Him through His life experiences. Jesus Christ, as the Son of God, was motivated by two inner motivators. Jesus Christ was led by the Spirit and moved by compassion. He understood His eternal purpose from the Father but had an inner compass to guide Him through His ministry. This is an important lesson for all of us who see Jesus Christ as the firstborn of many brethren. We all need to understand our Heavenly Father's guidance and work in our life to form us naturally and the place of the power of the Holy Spirit that is given to us in the appointed time.

It is important also to see how this fits into the eternal scheme of things. Jesus Christ not only had an earthly ministry but He also had an eternal one. His earthly journey prepared Him for His heavenly purpose as an intercessor for the people of God. As we go through life, we need to know we have someone who is making intercession for us who has been formed in His earthly life to be able to intercede for us with full understanding of the human condition.

> *Seeing then that we have a great High Priest who has passed through the heavens, Jesus the Son of God, let us hold fast our confession. For we do not have a High Priest who cannot sympathize with our weaknesses, but was in all points tempted as we are, yet without sin.* (Hebrews 4:14-15)

Like Jesus Christ the firstborn, you were formed for God's purpose both for now and for eternity. Don't fight with your past or with God, but find out what purpose God has established for you and look for how it can work for good.

This same principle also applies to history as a whole. I believe history is indeed "His" story, a story where everything works together for His purpose. Although not all things are instigated by God, all things are under His sovereign watch and can be utilized by Him for His purpose. God is the Creator and the Redeemer. The word ("redeem") means to (buy something back.) The near kinsman redeemer of the Old Testament had the right to buy back land and property sold by a family member so it was not lost to the family. Jesus Christ, our near kinsman redeemer, has certainly done that for us through His death. Not only does he cancel our debt but He buys back what we have lost. God, the redeemer of the earth, has carefully redeemed everything that pertains to His purpose so that we can have our choices and opportunities to fail, and He can ultimately have His portion back!

> *But now, thus says the LORD, who created you, O Jacob, And He who formed you, O Israel: "Fear not, for I have redeemed you; I have called you by your name; You are Mine. When you pass through the waters, I will be with you; And through the rivers, they shall not overflow you. When you walk through the fire, you shall not be burned, Nor shall the flame scorch you.* (Isaiah 43:1-2)

Notice here how God walks with His people. He creates, He redeems, and then He stays with us to protect us. The truth is things that can destroy the ordinary person cannot harm the chosen ones of God. His hand of blessing is a hand to keep us from death, even though He may not spare us from the evil or from our experience. Isaiah even declares that others died or suffered for their sins while God may have spared us.

> *For I am the LORD your God, The Holy One of Israel, your Savior; I gave Egypt for your ransom, Ethiopia and Seba in your place. Since you were precious in My sight, You have been honored, And I have loved you; Therefore I will give men for you, And people for your life.* (Isaiah 43:3-4)

As a pastor, I have met many people who lived on the wild side of life. They document God's protecting hand, yet they have seen how that hand did not protect others. Perhaps you know someone who suffered from the consequences of hurtful living, yet you have seen God's hand of mercy on you. You may know someone who died from the lifestyle you lived, but you made it through! We thank you God for your mercy to your children. He has redeemed us from the life of destruction.

Many times we may even struggle with the idea that we went through what we did. We lament the lost years and even think how good it would be if God would have rescued us earlier. How much more effective our life could be! These are some of the issues we will discuss in this book. Our lack of understanding of God and His ways has caused us to misinterpret the events of our life and the events of history as God is accomplishing His eternal purpose. The first issue we must recognize is: God has a long range plan for us and for the earth. Remember, God is an eternal God. Time is not nearly as important to God as it is to us. This became especially true when man sinned and the penalty of death was put upon us. Our lives now have the limitation of time, and we are always working against the clock of time. God is not under that time constraint, and it is important to understand that from His perspective, neither are we.

Despite the failure of man in the garden, God created us to become creatures of eternity. Even though death entered the world through sin, it is important to understand the gift of God is eternal life. As a Christian, we must still see ourselves as sons created for eternity. You have an eternal purpose. This doesn't just mean your purpose has eternal implications. It means you are living forever, and this earthly life is only a small portion of your existence when you are a creature of eternity. As Jesus Christ Himself was prepared for His earthly ministry and His eternal purpose, we must recognize that God is doing the same thing in us. How our life is lived has eternal consequences dictating our purpose and function in the heavenly realm for eternity. Jesus said some of us would rule over cities based on the stewardship of our talents in this life. This is not only about what we do but who we are. I know as I get older, I am fifty-six at the writing of this book, I always wished I knew when I was young what I know today. Unfortunately, some of the lessons and even understanding of the Scriptures could have only come through life experiences.

I remember when I was forty years old thinking how I wished I knew at twenty-four, when I started the church, what I knew at forty. I remember talking to an older pastor about this. He said, "I remember when I was forty I thought those young guys in their twenties didn't know anything. Now that I am seventy, I realize I didn't know anything when I was forty!" I was put in my place.

Now, as an elder to the body of Christ, I trust I have wisdom to disperse; but you and I must also realize we have something to offer eternity. Eternity isn't about learning how to play a harp while we are sitting on our cloud for eternity. Eternity is about learning how to rule and reign with Christ. Do you have the faith to believe in the eternal realm?

> *They shall see His face, and His name shall be on their foreheads. There shall be no night there: They need no lamp nor light of the sun, for the Lord God gives them light. And they shall reign forever and ever.* (Revelation 22:4-5)

The life of Jesus Christ exemplifies this concept. He lived thirty years in preparation for His earthly ministry. His earthly ministry lasted three years. His ministry was indeed glorious and must have been amazing to witness. The primary purpose of His ministry was eternal not earthly. His ministry prepared the way for His death. His death became the propitiation, or price, for our sins purchasing eternal life for us. At His resurrection He began His own eternal destiny; first, as the intercessor for all of us so we could reach our destiny in God, and finally, to sit as the King over all things!

Now as we look at God's eternal plan for mankind, we can see our misunderstanding as to how God does what He does. This will also help explain to us God's response to mankind as a whole. Because God is not looking for immediate results, we must understand God has a time frame within which results will occur. His plan is spread out over time, so we must be aware of the times and the seasons of God. The time or season will change the expectation God has for us.

> *To everything there is a season, A time for every purpose under heaven: . . . What profit has the worker from that in which he labors? I have seen the God-given task with which the sons of men are to be occupied. He has made everything beautiful in its time. Also He has put eternity in their hearts, except that no one can find out the work that God does from beginning to end.* (Ecclesiastes 3:1, 9-10)

This concept can also help us understand the beauty of the season even though it doesn't offer the optimum results. When looking at the seasons in the natural, we can see the purpose of winter, spring, summer, and fall. I live in the state of Michigan in the USA. Each season for us is distinct and can be seen for its individual purpose and beauty. Fall is a fruitful time in most places, but the fruitfulness can only happen properly if the other seasons provide their contribution. The moist rains of spring in our area provide the start while our warm summer provides optimum growth. The fall in turn provides the fullness of the bountiful harvest especially for the fruit on the trees. Even winter has its place and provides an opportunity for nature to bring the death of the things planted for the time of spring which is to come. Winter also offers the pruning of the unhealthy and inferior to guarantee the best will carry forth into the next generation. God has a time for everything. Even the coming of Jesus Christ, as the Savior of the earth, had an appointed time.

> *Even so we, when we were children, were in bondage under the elements of the world. But when the fullness of the time had come, God sent forth His Son, born of a woman, born under the law, to redeem those who were under the law, that we might receive the adoption as sons.* (Galatians 4:3-5)

Now we must ask ourselves the question: Did Jesus Christ come to the earth because of the fall of man, or was it a part of God's plan from the beginning? We must go to the Scriptures for our answer.

> *All who dwell on the earth will worship him, whose names have not been written in the Book of Life of the Lamb slain from the foundation of the world.* (Revelation 13:8)

> *For we who have believed do enter that rest, as He has said: "So I swore in My wrath, 'They shall not enter My rest,'" although the works were finished from the foundation of the world.* (Hebrews 4:3)

Not only was the Lamb slain before the foundation of the world but all the works of God were finished before the foundation of the world. Jesus, obviously, did not come to the earth because of the fall of man but because of the plan of God from the beginning. Those who are in the plan were also appointed before the foundation of the world.

> *It was granted to him to make war with the saints and to overcome them. And authority was given him over every*

tribe, tongue, and nation. All who dwell on the earth will worship him, whose names have not been written in the Book of Life of the Lamb slain from the foundation of the world. (Revelation 13:7-8)

Evil will befall the earth; but those written in the Book of Life, God's history book, will find God is looking out for them, and they will have a meeting place with destiny. This understanding will bring us to the place of rest spoken of in the Scriptures. It is a rest firmly rooted in the fact that God is the almighty and sovereign God and we, His people, are simply walking out the divine plan He has for us. We don't have to make it happen we simply have to let it happen. We must also let God work in us to will and to do His good pleasure.

> *Therefore, my beloved, as you have always obeyed, not as in my presence only, but now much more in my absence, work out your own salvation with fear and trembling; for it is God who works in you both to will and to do for His good pleasure.* (Philippians 2:12-13)

We are always anxious and in a hurry. We want things to happen, and we want them to happen now. God wants everything to be perfect according to His plan, so He patiently waits for the earth to bring forth its fruit. Like a farmer who has planted his seeds, God waits for the fruit to come forth from His labor.

> *Therefore be patient, brethren, until the coming of the Lord. See how the farmer waits for the precious fruit of the earth, waiting patiently for it until it receives the early and latter rain. You also be patient. Establish your hearts, for the coming of the Lord is at hand.* (James 5:7-8)

God is not waiting for things to get so bad that He needs to put in place a rescue plan. Through the mouth of the prophets, from the beginning, God has declared His intent for the earth and for man. Unfortunately, it seems the church has been waiting for the wrong things. Because the general perception of history is based on man's response to God rather than God's response to man, we have the idea that, in the end, God will just have to push us out of the way and rescue us from the overwhelming evil of the time. God's Word, on the other hand, has been God's declaration of His intent. This declaration states that in the end we will see the fulfillment of all things spoken by the mouths of the prophets.

> *Yet now, brethren, I know that you did it in ignorance, as did also your rulers. But those things which God foretold by the mouth of all His prophets, that the Christ would suffer, He has thus fulfilled. Repent therefore and be converted, that your sins may be blotted out, so that times of refreshing may come from the presence of the Lord, and that He may send Jesus Christ, who was preached to you before, whom heaven must receive until the times of restoration of all things, which God has spoken by the mouth of all His holy prophets since the world began.* (Acts 3:17-21)

God has a great plan, and you are a part of the plan. In this plan, you and I will be participants in a glorious company of people chosen by God, justified by His Son, and brought to glory by the work of the Holy Spirit in our lives. Jesus started something that will not be fully realized until the chosen ones of God come to the place of obedience and maturity demonstrated in the life of Jesus Christ! Why do I know these things will come to pass despite the evidence to the contrary? I know because I am convinced more of the power of God to impact "history" for His purpose than the weakness of man to hinder it.

> *What then shall we say to these things? If God is for us, who can be against us? He who did not spare His own Son, but delivered Him up for us all, how shall He not with Him also freely give us all things?* (Romans 8:31-32)

If we want to relate to God in His eternal purpose, we have to understand something about ourselves. In our natural state, we are not created with a full capacity to relate to eternal things. This is why it is important to understand how things were in the beginning. In chapter 2 of this book, I explained that death was in the plan and that God just provided the antidote, the Tree of Life. Eternal life was never natural; and just as it was in the beginning, we must come to the source of life, Jesus Christ, and partake of the life He has for us. But as noted in Ecclesiastes, God has put eternity in our hearts. Something inside of us longs for eternity. Even people outside the Christian church are often mesmerized by stories about heaven and eternity. We have eternity in our hearts for a reason, and we must develop what God has given us so our images of eternity are not born from human aspirations and desires but from God.

This is why in the past our thoughts about eternity and heaven are so filled with human aspirations. When the Scripture describes heaven as a place of gold and precious things, we have the idea heaven is about us instead of God. When surveyed about heaven, most people think of it as the place where you finally get what you want. In this life you give God what He wants, and when you get to heaven you will get rewards based upon how much you gave God what He wanted. I have news for you, heaven is not about us; it is about God. One day I was reading the Scriptures, and they talked about the eternal kingdom as a place where nursing children will, "play by the cobra's hole, and the weaned child shall put his hand in the viper's den." My problem with this Scripture is that I don't want snakes in heaven. I don't like snakes or reptiles. It was then God spoke to me and said, "Heaven won't be heaven because it will be everything you want; heaven will be heaven because you will be everything I want!" It is time to give our hearts to God and His eternal plan letting God conform our hearts and minds to His purpose and not our own.

In Summary

Since God is Alpha and Omega, the Beginning and the End, we must assume through His foreknowledge He knew of our choices. God's plan is gradual in order to give us the time necessary to conform to His plan and to recover from our failures as we respond to His plan. This should give us hope for ourselves individually when we make mistakes, but it should also fill us with love and admiration for a God who loves us so much He has made a great effort to allow us to be a part of His plan.

As Christians, we are not a religious group as the world would classify us. We are the sons of God; we are the family of God. God is our Father. From this perspective, we can see God as a loving and caring Father who has been nurturing and training us for His eternal purpose. Like the firstborn Son, our life from our nativity has had meaning and purpose. All things have been working toward the goal of God being manifested and glorified through us. We all need to understand our Heavenly Father's guidance and work in our life to form us naturally and the place of the power of the Holy Spirit that is given to us in the appointed time. We were formed for God's purpose both for now and for eternity.

Jesus died on the cross to be our redeemer. Not only does he cancel our debt but He buys back what we have lost. God, the redeemer of the earth, has carefully redeemed everything that pertains to His purpose so that we can have our choices and opportunities to fail, and He can ultimately have His portion back! Despite the failure of man in the garden, God created us to become creatures of eternity. How we live our lives has eternal consequences dictating our purpose and function in the heavenly realm for eternity. Eternity is about learning how to rule and reign with Christ. We must understand heaven is about God not us.

Chapter Six

WHERE DOES YOUR NATURAL LIFE FIT INTO HIS ETERNAL PLAN?

However, the spiritual is not first, but the natural, and afterward the spiritual. (1 Corinthians 15:46)

This Scripture reveals a very important order established as part of God's eternal plan and purpose. Here, God clearly states that the natural is a part of His spiritual plan for the world and for us as individuals. God establishes His plan in the natural then builds by adding the spiritual component. Ultimately, the glory of God is revealed through both the natural and the spiritual realm coming together in unity. This is true of His plan for planet Earth and for your life. The eternal plan for earth begins to unfold for us in the book of Genesis chapter 1. In the beginning, God created the heavens and the earth. Literally, the earth is a stage set up by God to demonstrate His wisdom, not just to the creatures of this new creation but to the whole heavenly realm. You are part of the cast.

> *and to make all see what is the fellowship of the mystery, which from the beginning of the ages has been hidden in God who created all things through Jesus Christ; to the intent that now the manifold wisdom of God might be made known by the church to the principalities and powers in the heavenly places, according to the eternal purpose which He accomplished in Christ Jesus our Lord,* (Ephesians 3:9-11)

The plan was formulated before the world was created. There is an appointed time for this plan to be revealed to the sons of man. God keeps His plans under wraps until the time appointed for us to know and to be a part of the plan. Through the natural order, God will demonstrate His glorious wisdom to the spiritual realm. Many Christians spend a lot of time trying to understand and even manipulate the spiritual realm. We often call it spiritual warfare when it is, in fact, carnal meddling. The beings of the spiritual realm are observers of the natural order, and we are called to be witnesses to them. Even our suffering can be a part of the unique testimony to them of God's glory.

> But recall the former days in which, after you were illuminated, you endured a great struggle with sufferings: partly while you were made a spectacle both by reproaches and tribulations, and partly while you became companions of those who were so treated; for you had compassion on me in my chains, and joyfully accepted the plundering of your goods, knowing that you have a better and an enduring possession for yourselves in heaven. (Hebrews 10:32-34)

The word "spectacle" here is from an original word in the Greek language for a theatre or place of public show. These Scriptures speak of the frequent suffering ministers of the gospel have endured over the years. Although we cannot always see the spiritual side of these conflicts, the real issue is not how we relate to the spiritual realm but what our life demonstrates in the natural to reveal the wisdom and power of God.

The story of Job gives us great insight into this process. Job's story begins with a dialogue between God and satan over the powerful witness Job is for God. God calls Job a perfect man and is very proud of his testimony. He even brags about Job to satan. This is a picture of what God is looking for in the world today. He is looking for the sons of God in the earth who will give Him bragging rights that He can declare to the spirit realm regarding our testimony. From a human perspective, this story seems dismal at best. With so much pain and suffering, his life has become a coined phrase, "the suffering of Job," when describing a very hard life.

As you watch the story of Job unfold, you will notice the activity of the spiritual realm; but Job himself is never given the insight into what was going on. It really wasn't necessary because the real story was how Job would respond in the natural, not how he would try to be involved in the spiritual realm. In the end, what was important in this story was what Job knew and declared about God. Job's friends, on the other hand, are rebuked by God because they did not speak what was right concerning God. When Job got through his struggle, his reward was not just spiritual, but it was natural. God not only returned to Job what he had lost, He doubled it! The double portion, according to the Scriptures, is the inheritance of the firstborn. It is this portion God ultimately wants to give to all His children.

> *The Spirit Himself bears witness with our spirit that we are children of God, and if children, then heirs — heirs of God and joint heirs with Christ, if indeed we suffer with Him, that we may also be glorified together. For I consider that the sufferings of this present time are not worthy to be compared with the glory which shall be revealed in us.* (Romans 8:16-18)

Unfortunately, this inheritance will only go to those who are willing to suffer for it! I know the church erred at one time when it almost glorified suffering. We needed to get over the glorifying of suffering, but we have come to the place where many people think of suffering only as a punishment. As a result, we have not given suffering the value it deserves. Many of the things we need to accomplish in life will require a certain level of suffering. The self discipline we must endure to be trained for our goals in life is, in a sense, suffering in the short term for the long term goal. Often, in our lives, the right choices we need to make come at the expense of personal desires and even pleasure. Everyone will tell you that true success in life will require a certain amount of pain and suffering. There was a time when I joined a gym to get in shape. My trainer said, "no pain, no gain." Like the majority of people I didn't last at the gym. The apostle Paul told his mentor, Timothy, *"bodily exercise profits a little."* I decided it was too little gain for the work required. But when it comes to the things of God, I want to follow the admonition of the Scriptures and be willing to "suffer in the flesh."

> *Therefore, since Christ suffered for us in the flesh, arm yourselves also with the same mind, for he who has suffered in the flesh has ceased from sin, that he no longer should live the rest of his time in the flesh for the lusts of men, but for the will of God.* (1 Peter 4:1-2)

Jesus is our example. Jesus had to suffer in the flesh to accomplish His eternal purpose. It was through the suffering of the flesh He was able to defeat satan and give us the opportunity to make a spoil of his goods.

> *having wiped out the handwriting of requirements that was against us, which was contrary to us. And He has taken it out of the way, having nailed it to the cross. Having disarmed principalities and powers, He made a public spectacle of them, triumphing over them in it.* (Colossians 2:14-15)

Of course, the cross became the greatest spiritual triumph of all times. But in fact, it was through a natural process of human pain and suffering that Jesus was able to accomplish this. The garden of Gethsemane was the precursor to this event. Remember, it was at Gethsemane that Jesus prayed that He would not have to go through the suffering of the cross. From a human perspective, it was a conflict of His flesh that caused Jesus Christ such pain in the garden. The pain was from His inner conflict of will and from the emotional stress created by dealing with the struggle at hand. He received spiritual help, but the choice and the action of obedience were made in the realm of the natural. This natural effort released the supernatural power available to us even in this hour. As Christians, we must understand God has created us as natural creatures, and it is mostly in this arena the power of God will be released. The principle of God says, first the natural then the spiritual.

Tithing is another example of this. Tithing was instituted in order to make provision for the house of God. It is a very natural principle to understand. Your money is used to pay the staff and to build and maintain buildings for the service of the ministry. We have no trouble handing out money we are asked to pay for the services we are rendered in life. That is until it comes to church! Then we get spiritual and judge the motivations of the church and the ministers. Many ministers and Christians are even embarrassed when the issue of money comes up. God is more practical. Through the prophet He declares, *"Bring all the tithes into the storehouse, that there may be food in my house."* If we will do this the Scripture continues to say, *"He will open for you the windows of heaven and pour out for you such blessing, that there will not be room enough to receive it."* The practical and natural act of giving releases the blessing of heaven!

With this in mind, we need to be careful not to think the spiritual realm cancels out the natural or is a way to circumvent it. This becomes very real when you witness the work of apostles and missionaries in church history. When a person goes to a new land, it can be very difficult. If it is a new land for the kingdom of God, it may also be very dangerous both from the threat of the people and the threat of natural forces like wild animals and disease. When you go to these lands, you must face the harsh reality that faith will not eliminate the struggles. Growing up in church we often heard about the miracles in foreign lands. This gives the impression it is a glorious work where faith has dispelled the normal obstacles of life. What actually happens is that those obstacles being faced present the setting for the release of the spiritual realm. The willingness to persevere in the struggle is what releases the power. This is why the apostle Paul declared:

> *strengthening the souls of the disciples, exhorting them to continue in the faith, and saying, "We must through many tribulations enter the kingdom of God.* (Acts 14:22)

The process and principle of the natural is very important to comprehend when surveying God's eternal plan. In the beginning, when God created man, He created us first from the natural realm not the spiritual. In the beginning, man was formed from the dust of the earth. God breathed in man "the breath of life." This God breath separated us from the rest of the animal kingdom giving us a unique place in the purpose of God. This God breath is the candle of the Lord. Through the God breath, or human spirit, we have an awareness of God and the capacity for self reflection. We need to keep ourselves aware of God and be mindful of our motivations concerning who God has made us to be. Yet, God created our natural man first. From the beginning, God intended us to be much more than natural creatures; but there is a reason God has chosen the natural man to be first. After the natural man, Adam, God sent the last Adam, Jesus Christ. Adam was a living being. Yet from the beginning, God planned on us being and having much more. When God added Jesus Christ, the last Adam, He was not just a natural being but a Life-Giving Spirit.

> *It is sown a natural body, it is raised a spiritual body. There is a natural body, and there is a spiritual body. And so it is written, "The first man Adam became a living being." The last Adam became a life-giving spirit. However, the spiritual is not first, but the natural, and afterward the spiritual. The first man was of the earth, made of dust; the second Man is the Lord from heaven.* (1 Corinthians 15:44-47)

Remember, Jesus Christ was a part of the plan from the beginning not just an afterthought. God intended to start with the natural and from this natural realm eventually bring forth the spiritual. The time frame was set before the earth was created, so we must assume God in His foreknowledge and wisdom had a reason for starting with the natural and then adding the spiritual part so many years later! We need to, at this juncture, dispel a common human assumption about God's plan. God doesn't stop and start His plan based upon the human response. As mentioned in an earlier chapter, we call the Genesis story the "fall" of man. Was it the fall or was it just the beginning? I propose we see it as the beginning with God planning to add the part lacking in His appointed time. He wanted us to see the natural shortcomings when we are without the Life-Giving Spirit, but it was all in the plan. Without God, the natural is not enough; with God, the natural will fulfill the divine plan. Now the spiritual does not circumvent the natural. It comes after the natural has developed to the point God intends, then He adds the spiritual. It is a compliment not a substitute. After we experience the natural life, God will add the supernatural life. God started with a living being but later added the Life-Giving Spirit. Through Adam, we experience life and death; but through Jesus Christ, the last Adam, we can experience eternal life.

The Life-Giving Spirit is the Holy Spirit. The human spirit serves an important part of who we are, however, the human spirit is a part of who we are in our natural state. The first Adam had a spirit from God. The human spirit makes us aware of God but also makes us aware of self.

> *The spirit of a man is the lamp of the LORD, Searching all the inner depths of his heart.* (Proverbs 20:27)

When we receive the Holy Spirit, our natural man has the connection to God that will enable us to truly be the sons of the living God. The Holy Spirit searches the things of God and brings them to the deepest part of our inner man.

> *But God has revealed them to us through His Spirit. For the Spirit searches all things, yes, the deep things of God. For what man knows the things of a man except the spirit of the man which is in him? Even so no one knows the things of God except the Spirit of God.* (1 Corinthians 2:10-11)

God follows the same process when bringing forth His sons in the earth. First, we are born in the natural. Later, in God's appointed time, God calls us to Himself in a more intimate experience. Through this experience, we are born again. We are now born from heaven not just born from the earth. We must always remember who and what we are in the natural is a part of God's plan for us and not a hindrance. Even the timing of what we would experience in the natural life is a part of the equation. When speaking of God's choosing of us for His eternal purpose, Jesus made a clear statement we must all understand.

> *No one can come to Me unless the Father who sent Me draws him; and I will raise him up at the last day. It is written in the prophets, 'And they shall all be taught by God.' Therefore everyone who has heard and learned from the Father comes to Me.* (John 6:44-45)

Before you ever came to God, you were already hearing from Him and being taught by Him. Isn't that amazing? We always put so much on ourselves after we become a believer. Yet, before you even knew it, God was at work in your life. Should it be that hard for us when God is so powerfully engaged in our lives? If God did a great work to lead us to Him, shouldn't we expect even greater after we have come to an awareness of Him? The Scriptures tell us how God loved us as sinners and how we should see His work in our lives as evidence of a more powerful proof of His love.

> *But God demonstrates His own love toward us, in that while we were still sinners, Christ died for us. Much more then, having now been justified by His blood, we shall be saved from wrath through Him.* (Romans 5:8-9)

This is the love of a Father for His son. He chose us in Christ before the foundation of the world. When we were conceived in our mother's womb, He intricately wove the tapestry of our person.

For You formed my inward parts; You covered me in my mother's womb. I will praise You, for I am fearfully and wonderfully made; Marvelous are Your works, And that my soul knows very well. My frame was not hidden from You, When I was made in secret, And skillfully wrought in the lowest parts of the earth. Your eyes saw my substance, being yet unformed. And in Your book they all were written, The days fashioned for me, When as yet there were none of them. (Psalm 139:13-16)

Once you came into the world, God fashioned your days. Why? He was using the natural circumstances of life to form you into the vessel of honor He has chosen you to be. I think it is important here to see His hand in the natural realm. He obviously formed us from the genes of our parents and used the people in our lives as a part of the process. God does not create and form us **outside** of our circumstances but **in** them. After we are born again, the principle is still at work. He allows things to be a part of us and our lives, we perhaps don't like or wish He hadn't, in order to form us into the spiritual creatures He intended us to be. We are spiritual creatures intricately entwined in the natural world!

I see the story of the beginning from the perspective of heaven. God started with a natural man and allowed both mistakes and failures to be a part. The consequences of those actions were necessary because we must follow the order God has made from the beginning. But I also see how God has worked with mankind over the ages, slowly introducing His plan without violating the natural order He established. The Bible is the record of His interactions with us that have been progressive in nature. Everything has been beautiful in it's time and marches forward with God managing both the past and the future. Some of God's dealings with mankind have followed the natural development of man over time. When mankind was in its early stages, God allowed things that were not a part of His desire for us but that would in time give Him an opportunity to introduce another aspect of His plan as we were ready for it. When the times of change come, God sets a higher standard for the time.

> *God, who made the world and everything in it, since He is Lord of heaven and earth, does not dwell in temples made with hands. Nor is He worshiped with men's hands, as though He needed anything, since He gives to all life, breath, and all things. And He has made from one blood every nation of men to dwell on all the face of the earth, and has determined their preappointed times and the boundaries of their dwellings, so that they should seek the Lord, in the hope that they might grope for Him and find Him, though He is not far from each one of us;* **Truly, these times of ignorance God overlooked, but now commands all men everywhere to repent,** (Acts 17:24-30)

This is the way we should look at our lives and the lives of others. It is no different than the pattern of the family where we give children time to grow, learn, and develop. As time and opportunities come, we expect more of them. This is how the heavenly Father works. To see this truth, we must recognize God is not just working with His people but with everyone. He doesn't just set the boundaries for His people but for all people. His people are the focus but not the only part.

> *When the Most High divided their inheritance to the nations, When He separated the sons of Adam, He set the boundaries of the peoples According to the number of the children of Israel. For the LORD's portion is His people; Jacob is the place of His inheritance.* (Deuteronomy 32:8-9)

When speaking to His people through the prophets, God made it very clear the other nations were used by Him for His purpose. Yet, He also emphasized the fact that in the end they too were held to the standard of His divine justice.

> *And this whole land shall be a desolation and an astonish-*
> *ment, and these nations shall serve the king of Babylon sev-*
> *enty years. 'Then it will come to pass, when seventy years are*
> *completed, that I will punish the king of Babylon and that*
> *nation, the land of the Chaldeans, for their iniquity,' says the*
> *LORD; 'and I will make it a perpetual desolation.* (Jeremiah
> 25:11-12)

The Babylonians were a bloodthirsty and conquering people.
When they came against His people, God gave His people into
their hand to fulfill His judgment on them. Afterward, He fully
punished the Babylonians for their wicked treatment of His people.
Everyone is accountable to God and used for His divine purpose.
This also demonstrates how God works through the natural order,
always mindful of the important principles He has ordered for
mankind.

God dealt with the natural man over many years time. One
day He came to the man Abraham and introduced the walk of faith
to Him. From his walk of faith, God produced a people for Himself. These people were set apart for God and demonstrated the
love and profound desire God had for a people called after His
name. The Scriptures tell us that all that was recorded about this relationship was given for our example and admonition. Isn't it amazing how much time and care God commits to His purpose in the
earth? Yet, we must understand this picture is still a picture of the
natural order. Israel is called by God; but they are the natural and
fleshly beginning, setting the foundation for the spiritual work
which is to come.

> *For I could wish that I myself were accursed from Christ for*
> *my brethren, my countrymen according to the flesh, who are*
> *Israelites, to whom pertain the adoption, the glory, the*
> *covenants, the giving of the law, the service of God, and the*
> *promises; 5 of whom are the fathers and from whom, ac-*
> *cording to the flesh, Christ came, who is over all, the eternally*
> *blessed God. Amen.* (Romans 9:3-4)

93

> *For if God did not spare the natural branches, He may not spare you either.* (Romans 11:21)

Many people are confused about how Israel fits into the plan of God. When you look at it from the divine principle, it is easy to see. The principle is first the natural then the spiritual. The natural certainly is important, but it can only continue as the plan of God if it goes through the process of the second birth creating the spiritual man. A natural Jew is a blessed person, but the blessing can only reach its fullness if they go on to the place of accepting the spiritual plan of God.

> *But it is not that the word of God has taken no effect. For they are not all Israel who are of Israel, nor are they all children because they are the seed of Abraham; but, "In Isaac your seed shall be called." That is, those who are the children of the flesh, these are not the children of God; but the children of the promise are counted as the seed. For this is the word of promise: "At this time I will come and Sarah shall have a son.* (Romans 9:6-9)

As a people, the seed of Abraham have not been discarded. God is faithful, and the word He has promised will always come to pass; but the eternal seed is the seed born of faith.

> *I say then, has God cast away His people? Certainly not! For I also am an Israelite, of the seed of Abraham, of the tribe of Benjamin. God has not cast away His people whom He foreknew. Or do you not know what the Scripture says of Elijah, how he pleads with God against Israel, saying, "LORD, they have killed Your prophets and torn down Your altars, and I alone am left, and they seek my life"? But what does the divine response say to him? "I have reserved for Myself seven thousand men who have not bowed the knee to Baal." Even so then, at this present time there is a remnant according to the election of grace.* (Romans 11:1-5)

Following this principle, we can certainly see the faithfulness of God being manifested in the events of history today in the Middle East. The Promised Land is still in the news as the world watches and debates the merits of the promise in modern times. Yet for us who know the Scriptures, it is a witness of the Word of God through God's promise to Abraham and the words spoken by the mouths of the prophets those many years after.

Just as we see God's wisdom in the overall plan for man, we need to see how these principles work in us as individuals. When we come into this world, our beginning starts in the natural realm. We are born of the flesh. Everything about our natural man will be a part of the end purpose and will demonstrate His glory and mercy to us. God will build upon this foundation with a spiritual dimension after we are born again, through faith, following the example of Abraham, our Father. We are born first of the man, Adam, then we must be born again through the second Adam, Jesus Christ, and be transformed by His Life-Giving Spirit. Then, we are not just alive but we are a part of the eternal purpose of God.

> *And so it is written, "The first man Adam became a living being." The last Adam became a life-giving spirit. However, the spiritual is not first, but the natural, and afterward the spiritual. The first man was of the earth, made of dust; the second Man is the Lord from heaven. As was the man of dust, so also are those who are made of dust; and as is the heavenly Man, so also are those who are heavenly.* (1 Corinthians 15:45-48)

Once we have received the Life-Giving Spirit, our natural life can be transformed, and we can become the person God has called us to be from the foundation of the world.

The experience of receiving the Holy Spirit is more than just becoming spiritually alive. This happens when we open our heart to God and receive His plan for our lives. Once we are made spiritually alive, we must see the need for empowerment from God. I know many Christians believe they receive the fullness of the Spirit when they are born again. We need to see the greatness of the move of God in the earth today if we want to be a part of the continuous plan of God. This movement is clearly indicated by the 500 million believers who have experienced this extra empowerment and can attest to the validity of it in their lives. I had a wonderful personal experience with Jesus Christ until, at age seventeen, I was baptized in the Holy Spirit. It did not discount my past experience, but it certainly added to it!

It is significant then to see how important the natural is to the spiritual. God wants to reconcile you as one new person both natural and spiritual just as He is doing in His plan concerning the natural and spiritual sons of Abraham.

> *For He Himself is our peace, who has made both one, and has broken down the middle wall of separation, having abolished in His flesh the enmity, that is, the law of commandments contained in ordinances, so as to create in Himself one new man from the two, thus making peace, and that He might reconcile them both to God in one body through the cross, thereby putting to death the enmity. And He came and preached peace to you who were afar off and to those who were near. For through Him we both have access by one Spirit to the Father.* (Ephesians 2:14-18)

This is the day when God wants to show His people how to reconcile the natural with the spiritual. There has long been an enmity between the natural and the spiritual. This is true in the big scheme and in our own personal lives. But now, through the power of the Life-Giving Spirit, God wants to reconcile this problem and bring forth the new man created after Christ in righteousness who will bring glory to His name! The Lord God, as our shepherd, guides and directs in both the natural and spiritual aspects of our life. He will do this until we arrive at the destiny we have as individuals. He will do the same for mankind as a whole.

In Summary

The natural world is part of God's spiritual plan. Through the natural order, God will demonstrate His glorious wisdom to the spiritual realm. He will reveal His plan at the appointed time. The real issue is not how we relate to the spiritual realm but what our life demonstrates in the natural to reveal the wisdom and power of God. God's reward is also both spiritual and natural. When we suffer loss, as in the story of Job, God not only returns what is lost but He doubles it. The double portion is the inheritance of the firstborn which goes to those who are willing to suffer for it. We don't want to glorify suffering nor do we want to think of suffering as only a punishment. Many of the things we need to accomplish in life will require a certain level of suffering.

We need to be careful not to think the spiritual realm cancels out the natural or is a way to circumvent it. Faith does not dispel the normal obstacles of life. What actually happens is that those obstacles being faced present the setting for the release of the spiritual realm. The willingness to persevere in the struggle is what releases the power. God starts with the natural and then brings forth the spiritual. Without God, the natural is not enough; with God, the natural will fulfill the divine plan. We must always remember who and what we are in the natural is a part of God's plan for us and not a hindrance. God's planning also includes those who do not receive Him. He uses them to fulfill His purpose. He doesn't just set the boundaries for His people but for all people. His people are the focus but not the only part.

God was involved in our lives before we became aware of Him. He chose us before the foundation of the world. He uses the natural circumstances of life to form us into the vessel of honor He has chosen us to be.

Chapter Seven

Did You Know Your Dominion Will Come Through Stewardship?

An important part of God's plan for mankind is dominion through stewardship. The revelation, or the unfolding of God's plan, begins in the book of beginnings, Genesis. What we see and understand concerning the beginning, will not only set the stage for what God is doing but will give us insight into what God intends or is going to do. As we already mentioned, we must see that in the beginning God created man in His image and likeness to take dominion and to subdue the earth. Mankind was told to be fruitful, multiply, fill up the earth, and take dominion. What an awesome plan God has for man! When we survey the human condition, it doesn't seem apparent that using people is a good idea. Sometimes, when we look at our lives, we have the same opinion. Certainly, God could have picked someone better to handle the things I have to deal with. From a human perspective, we think like the psalmist who saw so much more potential in the angels than in man.

> When I consider Your heavens, the work of Your fingers, The moon and the stars, which You have ordained, What is man that You are mindful of him, And the son of man that You visit him? For You have made him a little lower than the angels, And You have crowned him with glory and honor. You have made him to have dominion over the works of Your hands; You have put all things under his feet, (Psalm 8:3-6)

Of course, the great problem with us is that we always look at things from our perspective rather than God's. We do not have the confidence in God to trust His ability or His attitude towards us. Does God really think I can do this? Does God really have a plan that is taking me into consideration? These were the two issues facing Abraham and Sarah when God called them to walk with Him by faith. Each had to settle a different aspect of their fear. Abraham, as typical for men, was concerned about ability and power. His enablement came when he was convinced of the power available to him for the miracle only God could do.

> *And not being weak in faith, he did not consider his own body, already dead (since he was about a hundred years old), and the deadness of Sarah's womb. He did not waver at the promise of God through unbelief, but was strengthened in faith, giving glory to God, and being fully convinced that what He had promised He was also able to perform. And therefore "it was accounted to him for righteousness."* (Romans 4:19-22)

Sarah, on the other hand, as so often is the case with women, was more concerned about the personal implications. She seems aware of God's power, but her issue is about God's character and love for her. Could she trust God? Does God really care enough about her to make her a part of His plan? Her husband proved he was more concerned about getting the job done and getting what he was looking for. That is the reason why he was so willing to have a child by her handmaiden, Hagar. But God would have none of their carnal plan. God came to visit one day and talked to Sarah. She was even laughing within herself at the plan of God. God still insisted she would have a child, be a part of the plan of God, and see her heart's desire fulfilled. She would be a mother. When Sarah saw who God really was, she became empowered to fulfill His purpose.

> *By faith Sarah herself also received strength to conceive seed, and she bore a child when she was past the age, because she judged Him faithful who had promised.* (Hebrews 11:11)

After God created man and woman, they would have to confront these issues. God's plan for dominion involves a very important lesson exemplified in Genesis chapter 2. God's plan for us is dominion, but it starts with stewardship. God planted a garden and placed the man and woman in it. They were told to cultivate and protect this garden that God had for them. In church history, whenever the church had a glimpse of the dominion mandate God has given us, the thought was always to take over the world. We see dominion as an opportunity to seize or take control of something. God's design is dominion by stewardship. Take whatever God has placed in your hands and use it to its fullest potential. Guard and protect it because in the end it will produce what God has planned for you. Stewardship teaches us personal responsibility, yet, at the same time puts promotion and exaltation in the hands of God where it belongs. Many "dominionists" think it is the responsibility of the church to establish or enlarge the kingdom. Jesus Christ taught us that if we would be willing to die and give up our lives it would be the Fathers prerogative to "give" us the kingdom.

> *Do not fear, little flock, for it is your Father's good pleasure to give you the kingdom. Sell what you have and give alms; provide yourselves money bags which do not grow old, a treasure in the heavens that does not fail, where no thief approaches nor moth destroys. For where your treasure is, there your heart will be also.* (Luke 12:32-34)

The goal of the true believer is to press into the kingdom.

> *The law and the prophets were until John. Since that time the kingdom of God has been preached, and everyone is pressing into it.* (Luke 16:16)

After God gave the man and woman their garden, He placed a stipulation on their pleasure realm. They could enjoy all the trees of the garden except the tree of knowledge of good and evil, for in the day they ate of it they would surely die. For them, as is often the case with us, the temptation for the forbidden was always there. Ultimately, the temptation to eat of the tree was not for pleasure but for power. The serpent told them that if they ate of the tree they would be like God. The power would be in their hands. They decided that their best chance would be to take control of the situation. They were convinced they couldn't trust God's intent for them, and if the job was really going to get done, the power had to rest with them rather than with God. It was in this frame of thinking that the temptation of pleasure outside of God became more appealing than serving God. They ate of the tree of knowledge of good and evil, and judgment fell upon them. They were kicked out of the garden and would no longer have access to the tree of life.

It is very important we have a proper perspective of this story. There is a correction we need to make if we are to go to the place God has for us. We cannot see the story of the garden as the story of the "fall" of man. Instead, we must see this as simply a mistake by man. Although, according to the principle of stewardship, they experienced loss and judgment due to the transgression, the Scriptures do not call this a fall. That would give the impression we quit being what God created us to be, His children in the earth. It would also take away from the perspective of God's sovereignty saying that now man would no longer possess the ability to be what God created him to be. A proper perspective will allow us to set the appropriate expectation throughout our journey with God. Throughout church history, people who have seen this story as the fall have had their perspective colored concerning man and his place in the plan of God. Because this was referred to as the fall of man, we think we are no longer what God created us to be in the beginning. We also believe God's plan and purpose for the earth is a constantly changing plan based on our response to God. Our whole thinking, at best, has us groping to get back to the place we were at in the beginning of creation.

This theology has made the church a representation of a people always looking back. Jesus said, *"Remember Lot's wife."* What was her error? She looked back. Why were the Israelites always failing in the wilderness? They were always looking back. They were always remembering the good old days of the past and wanting to go back.

I was born in 1954 and was raised in church. One thing I always heard tell of was the talk about the good old days! The preachers were always talking about how bad sin was getting and how much better the Christians were in the past. In the Pentecostal church, the call was always to go back to the days of the New Testament church, placing a special emphasis on the book of Acts. These observations are more the yearning of the flesh than the burden of the Holy Spirit. As Christians, we should believe the best days are not the ones behind us but the ones in front of us.

> But the path of the just is like the shining sun, That shines ever brighter unto the perfect day. The way of the wicked is like darkness; They do not know what makes them stumble. (Proverbs 4:18-19)

As Christians, we should always see our path as getting brighter not darker.

> And so we have the prophetic word confirmed, which you do well to heed as a light that shines in a dark place, until the day dawns and the morning star rises in your hearts; (2 Peter 1:19)

The dark place should be the portion of the unrighteous. God wants us to receive the word of prophecy for this hour that will inspire us with hope for our future so we will arise and take our place in the world. Yes, darkness will cover the earth, but this is not supposed to be our motivation nor should it impact our expectation. As believers who understand the power of God and the fact He has an eternal plan that cannot be frustrated, we should move forward with great confidence in God and in our future!

> Arise, shine; For your light has come! And the glory of the LORD is risen upon you. For behold, the darkness shall cover the earth, And deep darkness the people: But the LORD will

arise over you, And His glory will be seen upon you. The Gentiles shall come to your light, And kings to the brightness of your rising. (Isaiah 60:1-3)

Jesus Christ did not say He would renovate or restore the church. He said He would build His church. The church He is building is going to be a victorious church, storming the gates of hell. This church will fulfill the prophecy spoken by God that the seed of the woman would put satan under their feet.

Jesus answered and said to him, "Blessed are you, Simon Bar-Jonah, for flesh and blood has not revealed this to you, but My Father who is in heaven. 18 And I also say to you that you are Peter, and on this rock I will build My church, and the gates of Hades shall not prevail against it. (Matthew 16:17-18)

Can we take Jesus at His word? Will we be like Adam and Eve in the beginning and think God is not able or God is unwilling to do what He has said He would do? The prophet Isaiah spoke of the coming Messiah and made a very important prophecy concerning Him:

For unto us a Child is born, Unto us a Son is given; And the government will be upon His shoulder. And His name will be called Wonderful, Counselor, Mighty God, Everlasting Father, Prince of Peace. Of the increase of His government and peace There will be no end, Upon the throne of David and over His kingdom, To order it and establish it with judgment and justice From that time forward, even forever. The zeal of the Lord of hosts will perform this. (Isaiah 9:6-7)

Notice that these Scriptures declare that of the increase of His government there will be no end. It is the zeal of the Lord that will perform it. Many times we see God's plan as one going up and down, going forward then falling back. The real problem is that we do not understand how God works, so we interpret His work through our own limited understanding. To understand the invisible God, the Bible tells us we should observe the natural, visible world He has created. God has instituted in His creation an important principle called seedtime and harvest. Remember, in the beginning, God placed man in a garden. The garden principle starts with a seed. The seed is planted and brings forth its fruit as gardening and the seasons do their work. As part of the work, during the winter season, the plants go through a process of death to prepare them for a greater harvest the next year. In the natural, many plants just cast forth their seeds, but for the farmer everything is based on the seedtime and harvest principle.

This is why, throughout the history of the Lord's dealings with the earth, it seems like things are rising then falling. We often trace the death process to human error when God uses it as His process. Remember, God factors in human failure as a part of His plan. So rather than seeing things as the fall of man, the fall of the church, or whatever fall you have witnessed in your life, we should see it as the process of seedtime and harvest knowing that death will always be a part of the process.

The life of Jesus Christ exemplifies this process. Jesus began His ministry after His baptism by John the Baptist and after being led into the wilderness to be tempted of the devil. He ministered for three years, and His ministry seemed to flourish and grow. Yet, He understood the principle of seedtime and harvest. He tried to teach this principle to His disciples, but in their carnal understanding they could not receive it. It happened nevertheless. Unfortunately for the disciples, their lack of understanding caused them great fear and much anxiety. This is what Jesus said concerning His impending death:

> But Jesus answered them, saying, "The hour has come that the Son of Man should be glorified. Most assuredly, I say to you, unless a grain of wheat falls into the ground and dies, it remains alone; but if it dies, it produces much grain. (John 12:23-24)

The glory comes after the death. Jesus Christ was first glorified after His death through resurrection, then through the birth of the church. The church has been through periods of flourishing, and at times it has appeared to die back or lose some of its luster. We should not see the story of Adam and Eve as a failed plan but as a seed planted leading to the glory of another day. Their seed, or their beginning, laid the foundation for phase one of God's plan awaiting the day the last Adam, Jesus Christ, would come and produce another type of seed and another dimension of God's plan.

We should see the work of God as an ongoing, growing, and prospering plan. This is why being a good steward of what God has put in your hands is so important. We may not know what God is doing or why, but when we accept that we are a part of God's plan we can take dominion of our portion so that God's eternal plan can prosper.

Just as the first Adam was told to multiply and fill up the earth, Jesus Christ commissioned His disciples to go into all of the world, preach the gospel, and disciple nations. The seed Jesus planted is under the same mandate of dominion and multiplication that God gave to Adam. God has a plan to fill the earth with His glory, and you must be convinced it will happen. The principle of God's kingdom is: He starts small, yet in the end it becomes the greatest and impacts the whole.

> *Another parable He put forth to them, saying: "The kingdom of heaven is like a mustard seed, which a man took and sowed in his field, which indeed is the least of all the seeds; but when it is grown it is greater than the herbs and becomes a tree, so that the birds of the air come and nest in its branches." Another parable He spoke to them: "The kingdom of heaven is like leaven, which a woman took and hid in three measures of meal till it was all leavened."* (Matthew 13:31-33)

We should quit looking back longing for what God has already done. We should look forward expecting even greater things. When the people of God were sent back to Jerusalem from Babylon, the work of God was continually stymied by the old folks who saw what God had done in the past. The prophet Haggai was raised up to encourage them and to cause the work of God to prosper again. He not only rebuked the nostalgia of the people but He also foretold of the great glory in front of them which continues in these latter days of time.

> For thus says the LORD of hosts: 'Once more (it is a little while) I will shake heaven and earth, the sea and dry land; and I will shake all nations, and they shall come to the Desire of All Nations, and I will fill this temple with glory,' says the LORD of hosts. 'The silver is Mine, and the gold is Mine,' says the LORD of hosts. 'The glory of this latter temple shall be greater than the former,' says the LORD of hosts. 'And in this place I will give peace,' says the LORD of hosts. (Haggai 2:6-9)

Many times we come to periods in our lives where the best seems to be in the past rather than the present. Some people never want to grow up, so they remain as children or long for days gone by. Many people after raising children think life leaves with the kids. Others are locked into their careers, and when the career is over life is over for them. As the children of God, we are children of eternity. There is still something for us to do, another purpose to fulfill. We need to look forward and not backward. Many times people make mistakes. To them, life is over or they think their fall has brought life to an end or has changed the plan of God. I don't always understand how He does it, but I do understand the principle. I will not limit God to my mistakes and failures or lack of proper choices. I will never second guess God, but I will always follow the admonition of the apostle Paul, both for myself and the body of Christ.

> Brethren, I do not count myself to have apprehended; but one thing I do, forgetting those things which are behind and reaching forward to those things which are ahead, I press toward the goal for the prize of the upward call of God in Christ Jesus. Therefore let us, as many as are mature, have this mind; and

if in anything you think otherwise, God will reveal even this to you. (Philippians 3:13-15)

Another aspect of the seedtime and harvest principle, involves the use of seasons to benefit the overall development of the fruit God is looking for. In the natural order, seasons can be very devastating as well as beneficial. I often watch nature shows that show this process in the wild. In northern climates, the cold winters wreak havoc on life where in other climates the long dry periods have the same impact. What happens during the severe times is the weeding out of inferior life to ensure only the best possible seed will go forth in the future. It is a cleansing and purifying time. The process of seedtime and harvest is also God's way of getting rid of the things that need to be removed from our lives. The word declares, *"whatever a man sows that he will also reap."* When the severe time comes, it is a time to reveal and remove the wrong things that are cluttering up God's perfect plan. The severe time will expose weaknesses as well as bad seed, removing them to insure a better future.

We see this process even in human created systems. It amazes me how God's order will always be seen, even when it involves something He has not necessarily instigated. The economic systems of the world will go through the seedtime and harvest principle also. When the severe times come, recession or depression, it will expose all behaviors that are a detriment to the system. In our country, we recently went through a difficult economic time. Our government, as well as a lot of people, lived like there was no tomorrow. Excessive debt, with no thought of the future, guided a people never satisfied. It guided a people who were always desirous of things they could not afford and unwilling to wait and save for the things they desired. It didn't seem the principle of sowing and reaping was true until the downturn came. Now many people and nations are in devastating situations that could have been avoided had they lived a principled life. Everyone experiences the severe times, but our behaviors make them easier or harder depending on what we have sown. If we are wise, we will take this time to set our houses and lives in order so we can continue to build for a better day.

God uses these severe times as times to purify His work from human works. God is building a holy habitation for Himself. This habitation cannot be the work of man but must be the work of God. Our endeavor should always be to walk in God's ways, but this doesn't always happen. So, God will use the severe season to eliminate human works that are contrary to His plan. Whereas the severe times wreak havoc on human effort, these times will always enhance what God is doing.

Now if anyone builds on this foundation with gold, silver, precious stones, wood, hay, straw, each one's work will become clear; for the Day will declare it, because it will be revealed by fire; and the fire will test each one's work, of what sort it is. If anyone's work which he has built on it endures, he will receive a reward. If anyone's work is burned, he will suffer loss; but he himself will be saved, yet so as through fire. (1 Corinthians 3:12-15)

The precious things of God actually forge through fire and pressure. The beauty of our precious jewels and energy sources to run our machines comes through a long and hardy process. We have tried to duplicate the divinely inspired natural processes but with only inferior results. We often try to do the same thing when we are working in God's kingdom. We try to make things happen fast, or we try to make things happen when it is not the right season. We often try to fulfill God's plans through our own devices and schemes. We may have temporary success, but time will eventually reveal the problem. Abraham and Sarah found this out when they tried to fulfill the promise God had given to them.

God had promised Abraham a son born from his seed. Sarah, his wife, suggested he take Hagar, her servant, and have a child by her. Surrogate mothers are nothing new. It was socially accepted and seemed to be successful when the child, Ishmael, was born. All went well until conflict arose between Sarah and Hagar. Human effort outside of God's Word will always produce flesh works. These works are listed in Galatians chapter 5 and certainly involve conflict and animosity. Eventually, the flesh works had to be removed so the true spiritual seed could prosper. Sooner or later the pure must come forth. This will often involve some difficulty in the process.

> *Now we, brethren, as Isaac was, are children of promise. But,*
> *as he who was born according to the flesh then persecuted*
> *him who was born according to the Spirit, even so it is now.*
> *Nevertheless what does the Scripture say? "Cast out the bond-*
> *woman and her son, for the son of the bondwoman shall not*
> *be heir with the son of the freewoman." So then, brethren, we*
> *are not children of the bondwoman but of the free.* (Galatians
> 4:28-31)

Because the process of God involves the human aspect, we know the plan will look sloppy to us. The beautiful thing for us is that God always has a redemption plan.

One of the names God ascribes to Himself is that He is the Lord our "Redeemer." In the Old Testament, when someone lost the family inheritance because of prodigal living, a near kinsman could buy back the inheritance. He became a redeemer of the inheritance. In this way, the penalty was paid for improper stewardship; but the inheritance would not ultimately leave the family. God's plan called for a penalty with correction for the loss. This is the pattern I see concerning God's dealings with His people. Sin must be atoned for; but in the end, God is always observing and redeeming the loss. This means that ultimately everything stays on course. God has a plan He initiated, and through His divine providence He keeps it on course so His purpose will be fulfilled. This is why, even in the midst of dire judgments, we should keep our focus on God's eternal plan with total confidence it will come to pass!

In Summary

An important part of God's plan for mankind is dominion through stewardship. The great problem with us is that we always look at things from our perspective rather than God's. God wants us to take whatever He has placed in our hands and to use it to its fullest potential. We need to guard and protect it because, in the end, it will produce what God has planned for us. Stewardship teaches us personal responsibility. Man fails when he gives in to the temptation to take control of a situation rather than trust God's intent for him.

We cannot look at the story of the garden of Eden as the fall of man. According to the principle of stewardship, they experienced loss and judgment due to their transgression; but the Scriptures do not call this a fall. To believe it was a fall, gives the impression that we quit being what God created us to be, His children in the earth. This belief would lead us to believe that God's plan for the earth is constantly changing based on our response to God. Instead we must see God's plan as a continually unfolding plan based on the principle of seedtime and harvest. The seed is planted and brings forth its fruit as gardening and the seasons do their work.

Death is part of the process. Although we do not like the thought of death, we have hope because glory comes after the death. We may not know what God is doing or why, but when we accept that we are a part of God's plan we can take dominion of our portion so that God's eternal plan can prosper. When we make a mistake we do not change the plan of God for us.

There is a principle of God that involves sowing and reaping. We may cause ourselves undue hardship or pain, but God uses these severe times to purify His work and to separate His work from that of human works. The precious things of God actually forge through fire and pressure. God's plan called for a penalty with correction for the loss. Sin must be atoned for; but in the end, God is always observing and redeeming the loss. We should keep our focus on God's eternal plan with total confidence it will come to pass!

Chapter Eight

Do You Understand Jesus Christ Is the Prototype for Your Life?

. . . as Moses was divinely instructed when he was about to make the tabernacle. For He said, "See that you make all things according to the pattern shown you on the mountain." (Hebrews 8:5)

In the Old Testament, God instructed Moses to follow a divine plan in the building of the tabernacle that would be their center of worship. This tabernacle was built from a heavenly pattern God showed him on the Holy Mountain. Incredibly, the Old Testament foundation the church is built upon was a prototype of what is taking place in the realm of heaven. This is an amazing concept. Before God initiated His ultimate plan, He instructed Moses to build a prototype to show us a pattern we are to follow. In an earlier chapter, I talked about God being a designer/builder. Now we see from the Scriptures, God also put together a prototype, so that when we do our part we can have a fully illustrated pattern to follow. In that sense, the garden of Eden was a prototype of the ultimate destiny revealed in Revelation 22. Even the history of the children of Israel, was written and given to us for our example or prototype. Unfortunately, it represents a "failure" prototype.

Now all these things happened to them as examples, and they were written for our admonition, upon whom the ends of the ages have come. (1 Corinthians 10:11)

To me, it is an amazing concept that God would spend so much time putting His plan together. He must be very fussy as to the details to spend so much time and effort bringing to pass His perfect plan. Many people do not understand God has an eternal plan. As a result of this error, they think the Bible is divided into eras where God basically tries something, and after it fails He tries something else. Others suppose God has done many different things just to show man how miserable he is, so God can come through in the end to rescue him. No, God has an eternal plan. He builds line upon line and principle or precept upon precept.

> *Whom will he teach knowledge? And whom will he make to understand the message? Those just weaned from milk? Those just drawn from the breasts? For precept must be upon precept, precept upon precept, Line upon line, line upon line, Here a little, there a little.* (Isaiah 28:9-10)

These Scriptures indicate God is not only building in a specific manner but He is developing His people one step at a time. His plan is to bring them to a mature state where they can accept their part in the plan and take responsibility for their part in the purpose of God.

God has a plan for each generation suitable for them and the time they live in. This is why the Scriptures declare that everything is beautiful in its time. The law of Moses and the plan the children of Israel were under was beautiful in its time, but when the new time came the people needed to respond to the new plan. Since each line of the plan is built on the other, it is very important we do not lose sight of the purpose of the plan that precedes the time we are living in. We know how the people refused the time when Jesus Christ came to them. Jesus was the fulfillment of all the hopes and prophecies of the old covenant, but the people were unwilling to respond to the new thing God had for them. I am sure it was because they had experienced the beauty and blessing of the earlier plan. We can't see them as evil people because it is normal to the human condition to refuse change when it comes. Jesus Christ Himself acknowledged this.

> *And no one puts new wine into old wineskins; or else the new wine will burst the wineskins and be spilled, and the wineskins will be ruined. But new wine must be put into new wineskins, and both are preserved. And no one, having drunk old wine, immediately desires new; for he says, 'The old is better.* (Luke 5:37-39)

Jesus recognized our resistance to new things. Although He understands our "immediate" response, it does not excuse us from being unwilling to receive what God has for us. We need to remind ourselves to be established in the "present truth" God is manifesting in the earth. I want you to understand that the new is not a new plan but a new level unfolding in the plan God had from the beginning.

> *Therefore, brethren, be even more diligent to make your call and election sure, for if you do these things you will never stumble; for so an entrance will be supplied to you abundantly into the everlasting kingdom of our Lord and Savior Jesus Christ. For this reason I will not be negligent to remind you always of these things, though you know and are established in the present truth.* (2 Peter 1:10-12)

Jesus not only spoke of the new wine but the new wineskins. Many times people will rejoice in the new wine, but then will resist the structural changes necessary to facilitate the new wine. When Jesus Christ came, He was very well received until the point of changing the structure of the religious system. All our structures must be seen as housing for the wine of God. When the wine changes, if you don't change the structure it will be damaged by the wine. Interestingly enough, when the wine of God's presence begins to burst the system, people will choose the safety of the system over the life of what God is doing. It seems in history that it is a rare thing for people to prefer the life of the "new wine" over the safety of the structure that has held it. Even our structures are beautiful in their time, but when change comes it must be a complete change. The children of Israel demonstrate this principle. Too often people fail to see the spiritual reality of the time. As God led the children of Israel, they often failed to see the spiritual aspect of their journey. For them, their journey did not have a spiritual component. They never could see what was really going on in their journey. They could only see their lives from a natural perspective. Consequently, they mostly lost out on what God had for them.

> *Moreover, brethren, I do not want you to be unaware that all our fathers were under the cloud, all passed through the sea, all were baptized into Moses in the cloud and in the sea, all ate the same spiritual food, and all drank the same spiritual drink. For they drank of that spiritual Rock that followed them, and that Rock was Christ. But with most of them God was not well pleased, for their bodies were scattered in the wilderness.* (1 Corinthians 10:1-5)

This was the same problem they had when Jesus Christ came to them. He was God coming in the flesh. Because they could not see past the natural, they were once again unable to enjoy the great provision God had for them. Jesus Christ, although God in the flesh, was also a prototype for us. Jesus Christ came to show us what it should be like as a man. He was the image of God.

> *He has delivered us from the power of darkness and conveyed us into the kingdom of the Son of His love, in whom we have redemption through His blood, the forgiveness of sins. He is the image of the invisible God, the firstborn over all creation.* (Colossians 1:13-15)

He came to show us what God would look like as a man because God's purpose is still the same as it was in the beginning. He wanted us to take our place of authority in His creation, and He wanted us to be "in His image." He would give us the image to behold so that in seeing Him we could become like Him.

> *Beloved, now we are children of God; and it has not yet been revealed what we shall be, but we know that when He is revealed, we shall be like Him, for we shall see Him as He is. And everyone who has this hope in Him purifies himself, just as He is pure.* (1 John 3:2-3)

In understanding our need to see Jesus Christ, I think we often do just the opposite of the people of God in the Old Testament. Whereas they were unwilling to see the spiritual side of their experience, we are often afraid or unwilling to see the natural side of Jesus Christ. Although we must firmly believe Jesus Christ was the image of God, we must also be mindful of His humanity. The Scriptures declare Him to be a man.

> *For there is one God and one Mediator between God and men, the Man Christ Jesus, who gave Himself a ransom for all, to be testified in due time,* (1 Timothy 2:5-6)

The Jewish people refused to believe a man could be the Son of God. They became so infuriated when He, as a man, claimed His association with divinity they sought to kill Him.

> *Your father Abraham rejoiced to see My day, and he saw it and was glad." Then the Jews said to Him, "You are not yet fifty years old, and have You seen Abraham?" Jesus said to them, "Most assuredly, I say to you, before Abraham was, I AM." Then they took up stones to throw at Him; but Jesus hid Himself and went out of the temple, going through the midst of them, and so passed by.* (John 8:56-59)

The heathens were just as opposed to this view as the Jews. The predominate philosophy of the time came from the Greeks. They were heavily influenced by Gnosticism. Gnosticism teaches us that the natural world is evil and only good things are spiritual things. Nothing good could come from the natural world; hence, Jesus Christ as a man could not be divine. Even Christians influenced by Gnosticism, concluded Jesus Christ may have appeared human; but this was only an appearance, not a reality. This is why it took the Christian church so long to reconcile the fact that Jesus Christ was truly God **and** truly man. Although this conclusion was scriptural, it was conflicting to the minds of people as it is even to this day.

We know from the Scriptures the conception of Jesus Christ was supernatural. Jesus Christ was conceived by the Holy Spirit and born of a virgin called Mary. However, everything surrounding His birth and His early life appeared very human and natural. After the initial confirmations from the angels and the three wise men, Jesus' life took a very normal turn. Very little of His early life was recorded by the gospels. We do learn that at age twelve He was highly motivated by His heavenly call. When His family was visiting Jerusalem for one of the feasts, He became lost. His parents found Him in the temple mesmerizing the people with His knowledge of the Scriptures. When he was scolded by His father He replied, *"Did you not know that I must be about my Father's business?"* Even with all the supernatural events of His birth, His parents did not understand the statement Jesus made. They obviously just corrected Him as any parent would, and Jesus submitted to the natural order.

> *Then He went down with them and came to Nazareth, and was subject to them, but His mother kept all these things in her heart. And Jesus increased in wisdom and stature, and in favor with God and men.* (Luke 2:51-52)

Many people have refused to see how normal and natural the life of Jesus Christ would have been. Some even found supposedly lost gospels to speculate that Jesus was a little superman as a child. This is not the story of the Bible. Jesus Christ had to live a very normal and often troubled life so He could be trained for the service

His Father had for Him. The prophet Isaiah foretold of His life and the pain He would endure for us in the natural realm of His life.

> *Who has believed our report? And to whom has the arm of the LORD been revealed? For He shall grow up before Him as a tender plant, And as a root out of dry ground. He has no form or comeliness; And when we see Him, There is no beauty that we should desire Him. He is despised and rejected by men, A Man of sorrows and acquainted with grief. And we hid, as it were, our faces from Him; He was despised, and we did not esteem Him. Surely He has borne our griefs And carried our sorrows; Yet we esteemed Him stricken, Smitten by God, and afflicted.* (Isaiah 53:1-4)

"Who has believed our report?" Isaiah knew by the Spirit of God how incredible the concept of the incarnation would be. Who would believe God would come to the world and grow up with pain and suffering? Who would believe it was God if He wasn't strong in stature and handsome? I know if I was God coming to the earth I would want to pick out the best attributes, not the worst. I would want both the stature and the looks. If I could pick out my temperament, I would want to have a happy disposition, not one of sorrow familiar with grief and sadness. Jesus didn't come to live a life for Himself. First of all, Jesus came so He could be familiar with the difficulties of the human condition. This would prepare Him for both His earthly and eternal purpose. He was to be a High Priest sympathetic to our needs. He also came to live a life of example. This "prototype" of the sons of God would have to face difficulty as a human being and be an overcomer in all things so we could know we also could be an overcomer like Him.

> *For we do not have a High Priest who cannot sympathize with our weaknesses, but was in all points tempted as we are, yet without sin. Let us therefore come boldly to the throne of grace, that we may obtain mercy and find grace to help in time of need.* (Hebrews 4:15-16)

Jesus Christ was tempted in all points like us. This means He was fully human and was tempted with the human condition. He was tempted but did not give in to His temptation.

Most people do not fully appropriate God's grace for their lives. Often it is because we do not understand the difference between mercy and grace. Grace is God's favor and graciousness towards us. Before we know the Lord, it would be impossible to choose to follow God. God chooses us; we don't choose Him.

> *You did not choose Me, but I chose you and appointed you that you should go and bear fruit, and that your fruit should remain, that whatever you ask the Father in My name He may give you.* (John 15:16)

We were dead in our trespasses and sins. Dead people can't help themselves. It is only God's grace, mercy, and favor that chooses us and releases us from the guilt and penalty of sin.

> *But God, who is rich in mercy, because of His great love with which He loved us, even when we were dead in trespasses, made us alive together with Christ (by grace you have been saved) For by grace you have been saved through faith, and that not of yourselves; it is the gift of God, not of works, lest anyone should boast. For we are His workmanship, created in Christ Jesus for good works, which God prepared beforehand that we should walk in them.* (Ephesians 2:4-5 & 8-9)

Notice this calling leads to good works we have been appointed for. Grace is not just God's unmerited favor we receive in the beginning of our relationship with Him. Grace is God's willingness to empower us to overcome every obstacle in life and ultimately to fulfill our Father's purpose for our life just like Jesus Christ, our example. Hebrews 4:14-15 tells us we need to come boldly to the throne of grace so we can receive mercy and grace to help us in our time of need. God wants to help us in our time of need. Often we only see grace from the perspective of mercy. Therefore, our idea is: "God get me out of here." To fulfill our Father's purpose, we must get to the place where we accept the challenges set before us and receive the help, God's grace, to get us through.

Jesus Christ is our example. In the garden of Gethsemane, He asked His Father to take the cup of suffering He was about to face away from Him. When He cried out, the Scriptures tell us God heard Him. This does not mean He was able to get out of the situation. It means He was empowered in the situation to face it.

> who, in the days of His flesh, when He had offered up prayers and supplications, with vehement cries and tears to Him who was able to save Him from death, and was heard because of His godly fear, though He was a Son, yet He learned obedience by the things which He suffered. And having been perfected, He became the author of eternal salvation to all who obey Him, (Hebrews 5:7-9)

Something happened to Jesus, the man, to cause Him to focus on the joy of the accomplishment rather than the pain of the ordeal.

> looking unto Jesus, the author and finisher of our faith, who for the joy that was set before Him endured the cross, despising the shame, and has sat down at the right hand of the throne of God. For consider Him who endured such hostility from sinners against Himself, lest you become weary and discouraged in your souls. You have not yet resisted to bloodshed, striving against sin. And you have forgotten the exhortation which speaks to you as to sons: "My son, do not despise the chastening of the LORD, Nor be discouraged when you are rebuked by Him; For whom the LORD loves He chastens, And scourges every son whom He receives." (Hebrews 12:2-6)

Jesus Christ was empowered to face the difficulty of the task, and we can be too. The word "chastening" here speaks not of punishment but of training. It is training that involves the discipline of putting someone in an uncomfortable situation if necessary and teaching them the discipline needed to accomplish their goals in life. This was true of Jesus Christ, and it is also true of us. He did for us what we could not do for ourselves to prepare us for the grace of enablement. The enablement is the ability to accomplish all God has for us. It is important to see this training is not just in the spiritual realm but also in the natural.

Many Christians see grace as God's sovereign choice for us of eternal salvation. To them, eternal life is the only issue so everything revolves around whether or not this will get me to heaven. Many other Christians see an extra help through the Holy Spirit. The Holy Spirit comes as a source of power to help us accomplish and receive all God has for us in this life. Most fail to recognize the fact that God wants us to be like Jesus. He wants us to make the Word a reality in our everyday life. He wants to train us as a person. God wants to develop us in character and in our person so that all areas of our life can bring glory to His name. The fruit of the spirit is when the work of God takes hold of our person and we begin to manifest God's character in our life. This is when the image and likeness of God will be manifested in His people. It is this mature people who will walk in the fullness God has for them.

Most people are more interested in personality than character. We enjoy the people whose personalities add to our enjoyment of life. Even when choosing leaders, people often are more interested in a person's personal charisma than the more important attributes of their character. If you were to judge, even Jesus Christ, on His personality you may not have liked Him. I know the images we often make up to portray Jesus Christ. Because He was love manifested, we picture someone who would always make us feel loved. Jesus would always say the right things and do the right things. We picture Him as the Lamb of God and that we should. Do you realize He is also the Lion of the tribe of Judah? As a lion, He could be pretty rough.

122

One day a woman approached Him to help her with her demon possessed daughter. Jesus responded, *"It is not good to take the children's bread and throw it to the little dogs."* This is hardly the response we would expect to hear from a loving person. When Jesus Christ is getting ready to face the cross, Peter, in love, says it won't happen. He obviously is speaking of his intent to help Jesus. How did Jesus respond? Jesus said, *"Get behind me, Satan, for you are not mindful of the things of God but the things of men."* I would guess Peter was more than a little offended with that remark!

When I was growing up, I didn't like rough or mean people. I made this opinion spiritual and always went out of my way to be nice. I really believed God had to be the nicest person of all because He was love, and if someone loves you they will certainly be nice to you. It took a long time for God to break my mindset, but I did find out in time that I was nicer than God. God is forever doing things I don't think are "nice." The Lion of the tribe of Judah is also the one who will judge sin and disobedience in the world. There is a time for nice and there is a time when Jesus will not be "nice."

Now I saw heaven opened, and behold, a white horse. And He who sat on him was called Faithful and True, and in righteousness He judges and makes war. His eyes were like a flame of fire, and on His head were many crowns. He had a name written that no one knew except Himself. He was clothed with a robe dipped in blood, and His name is called The Word of God. And the armies in heaven, clothed in fine linen, white and clean, followed Him on white horses. Now out of His mouth goes a sharp sword, that with it He should strike the nations. And He Himself will rule them with a rod of iron. He Himself treads the winepress of the fierceness and wrath of Almighty God. And He has on His robe and on His thigh a name written: KING OF KINGS AND LORD OF LORDS. (Revelation 19:11-16)

We can't make God who we want Him to be. God is the "I AM." God is who He is, and we must worship Him for who and what He is. If we are to be in His image, we can't serve a God who is the work of our hands. We must serve a God who has made us the works of His hand. God is molding and shaping you. You need to recognize what God is doing in your life, and you must recognize what He is doing in the earth. God does not just want us to be observers but great participants in His plan. He still wants to put His creation in our hands. We are destined to be the judges of the heavens and the earth.

> *Do you not know that the saints will judge the world? And if the world will be judged by you, are you unworthy to judge the smallest matters? Do you not know that we shall judge angels? How much more, things that pertain to this life?* (1 Corinthians 6:2-3)

If we are being molded and shaped, where is He taking us? This is what we will be looking at from this point on in this book.

In Summary

God has an eternal plan and He gives us specific instructions so we know how to carry it out. As with Moses and the building of the tabernacle in the Old Testament, God gives instructions so that His plan can be executed one step at a time. Through the process, we come to maturity and learn to take responsibility for our part in the purpose of God. The time of God is crucial. God has a plan for each generation suitable for them and the time they live in. We must be willing to change as the plan of God unfolds. Our human tendency is to resist change. Resisting change can cause us to miss the "present truth" God is manifesting in our generation. We must see past the natural and understand what God is doing in the spiritual. However, we must not reject what God uses in the natural to accomplish His purpose.

Jesus was our prototype. He was both God and man. He came to show us who God is. God wants us to be like Him. God wants to develop us in character and in our person so that all areas of our life can bring glory to His name. God is molding and shaping us. We need to recognize what God is doing in our lives. If we are to be in His image, we can't serve a God who is the work of our hands. We must serve a God who has made us the works of His hand.

Chapter Nine

IS IT POSSIBLE TO UNDERSTAND GOD AND WALK IN MATURITY?

Brethren, do not be children in understanding; however, in malice be babes, but in understanding be mature. (1 Corinthians 14:20)

When reading the Bible, it is always important to let the Bible interpret itself. No Scripture should be of a private interpretation but should be interpreted from the whole counsel of God. The scriptural precedent states that it should be out of the mouth of two or three witnesses. When we look at the book of Genesis, many people will look at chapters 1 and 2 as separate stories without tying the two together. Instead, we should see chapter 1 as a general description of creation with chapter 2 being an amplification of the plan God has for man. With this in mind, we must be careful to keep a consistency to the plan since God certainly does. In Genesis 1, God gives a clear picture of who man is and what His plan for man is.

Then God said, "Let Us make man in Our image, according to Our likeness; let them have dominion over the fish of the sea, over the birds of the air, and over the cattle, over all the earth and over every creeping thing that creeps on the earth." So God created man in His own image; in the image of God He created him; male and female He created them. Then God blessed them, and God said to them, "Be fruitful and multiply; fill the earth and subdue it; have dominion over the fish of the sea, over the birds of the air, and over every living thing that moves on the earth." (Genesis 1:26-28)

God created us in His image and likeness with a mandate of dominion. As I have mentioned, this theme continues and has been built upon by the coming of Jesus Christ to the earth bringing man's reconciliation to God. Jesus Christ came not as God interjecting something into history but as God proceeding with His story as planned. This reconciliation reestablished our relationship with God. This reconciliation also reconciled us to our purpose to be conformed to the image of Christ, who is the visible image of the invisible God. Moving forward to chapter 3, we see how man disobeyed God's commandment not to eat of the tree of knowledge of good and evil. In fulfillment of His promise of consequences for their disobedience to God, they were kicked out of the garden of Eden.

> *Then the LORD God said, "Behold, the man has become like one of Us, to know good and evil. And now, lest he put out his hand and take also of the tree of life, and eat, and live forever" — therefore the LORD God sent him out of the garden of Eden to till the ground from which he was taken. So He drove out the man; and He placed cherubim at the east of the garden of Eden, and a flaming sword which turned every way, to guard the way to the tree of life. (Genesis 3:22-24)*

God had told man that he would die when he disobeyed Him. To fulfill this promise, man had to be kicked out of the garden so he would not have access to the tree of life. According to the principle of sowing and reaping, we will always reap what we sow; but the impact is not always immediately felt. The Word may come to pass in the process of time. Many people think that if the immediate impact of our actions is not apparent, we have escaped the judgment of the Word. The consequence is a reality we will eventually face because the principles of God are everlasting.

I want to point out something interesting. God said, *"The man has become like one of us."* When taken in the context of the whole story, you will see this was God's plan from the beginning. God created us to be like Him. I propose that in the greater story of God, the issue for God was not that we would have the ability to discern good and evil but when and how this ability would come about. God's plan has a timetable and a pattern. Our mistakes will impact our lives but will never change God's plan. As we have seen, human effort makes God's plan messy from our perspective; but God always has a cleanup plan. This is why Romans 8 confidently affirms the inevitability of God's plan.

> *And we know that all things work together for good to those who love God, to those who are the called according to His purpose. For whom He foreknew, He also predestined to be conformed to the image of His Son, that He might be the firstborn among many brethren. Moreover whom He predestined, these He also called; whom He called, these He also justified; and whom He justified, these He also glorified. What then shall we say to these things? If God is for us, who can be against us? He who did not spare His own Son, but delivered Him up for us all, how shall He not with Him also freely give us all things? Who shall bring a charge against God's elect? It is God who justifies. Who is he who condemns? It is Christ who died, and furthermore is also risen, who is even at the right hand of God, who also makes intercession for us. (Romans 8:28-34)*

You are destined to glory! Can you imagine the price God paid for your glory? Jesus Christ, who died for you, ever lives to make intercession for you. He is pleading for you to continue on the journey so His Word will come to pass in your life. You have made some messes, but there is no condemnation for those who love Him and are called according to His purpose. You may suffer some loss and face some difficulties, but Jesus Christ will get you through. We need to understand God has a process that factors in human error. God wants you to find your place in Him so He can do the cleanup necessary for your purpose to come to pass. Now, I want you to look at the original plan from a different perspective to understand how God sees mankind and how He sees us as individuals.

When I see Genesis chapter 2 from God's eternal purpose, it changes the perspective considerably. Again, God's original plan was for man to take dominion as His sons in the earth. Although He makes us capable, we were not yet ready for the responsibility He has for us. It is just like in our human situation. When a child is born, it fully contains all the elements of its adult state; but it will take time for the development of the child both naturally and intellectually. That is why God has given us parents to guide us on the journey. Although the first man and woman were created in the adult stage of life, they would have required much training and development before they could have been fully given the charge God had for them. The garden of Eden was a safe place created by God for this process to unfold. God would not have given mankind a mandate of dominion over the planet and then place him in the garden to be sheltered forever from their destiny. The garden can easily be seen as a temporary home for the children until the time they would be sent forth to fulfill their destiny. God's separation of man from the tree of life was so they would not live forever in a state He did not intend for them to live in. He was like a Father saying, "I can't let you live here forever as a child; you need to go out and face life so you can grow up!" The same holds true for us today.

Nobody loved having children more than me. My wife and I loved being parents and loved every minute of our children's lives. We have the pictures and videos to show that we wanted to hold on to every memory. As much as we loved our children, however, it would have been very heartbreaking if they never grew up. The actions they displayed as children were so much fun, but it would be irritating if they continued those same actions as adults. Changing the diaper of an infant is much more tolerable than changing the diaper of an adult.

Do you realize God feels the same way? Many Christians refuse to grow up. Many even have a doctrinal belief that causes them to think God's intent was for us to stay in a state of innocence forever. We often think of heaven as a place of innocence and pleasure rather than the place of ruling and authority Jesus Christ spoke about in the parable of the talents. Do you see why it is so important that we change our doctrine to conform to concepts God intended us to walk in so that we can take our place of responsibility and authority?

Through the parable of the talents, Jesus Christ made it very clear that our actions here on earth would not just determine **where** we would spend eternity but **how** we would spend it. Some will be given rewards and authority, and others will be limited for eternity. The unfaithful steward in this parable suffered loss and was cast into the place of outer darkness. This was obviously a place of sadness and regret over how he had handled his stewardship!

With the tree of knowledge of good and evil in the garden, man was given an opportunity to learn and grow in time. We can learn through experience or through observation with instruction. The tree of knowledge of good and evil was not in the garden to tempt man but to give him an opportunity to learn through observation. I am sure you have heard the oft stated slogan, "experience is the best teacher." Experience can burn lessons deep in us, but they often require needless pain and suffering. The Scriptures teach us to learn from the experience of others. This is what the Bible is all about. If we learn through the observation of other people's lives, we can avoid their mistakes.

The Bible is a book of people making a lot of mistakes. Some people find encouragement from this, thinking that it gives them the right to make mistakes too. This is true, you make mistakes and God can forgive you. But wouldn't it be better to learn from the mistakes of these people so we can avoid their mistakes and costly consequences? Whatever a person sows that is what they will reap, so why seek the freedom to sow bad seeds when we can be guided by the instruction and experience of others? I, of course, am not advocating a mistake free life; but the Scriptures certainly advocate a life with fewer struggles when you follow God.

This is the pattern God has instituted. In the church and in the family, God ordains leaders to be responsible to teach and train the children of the house. A primary aspect of the training is for the leaders or parents to lead by example. Example becomes the most influential aspect of the training. Jesus Christ exemplified this when speaking of His own Father.

> *Then Jesus answered and said to them, "Most assuredly, I say to you, the Son can do nothing of Himself, but what He sees the Father do; for whatever He does, the Son also does in like manner.* (John 5:19)

I have found this to be the case with my children. Many of the attributes I have imparted to them have come more from my example to them than my actual instruction. This is why properly functioning churches and families are the key to producing the seed God is looking to produce in the earth. In the garden of Eden, Adam and Eve were not only forbidden to eat of the tree of knowledge of good and evil, they were also offered the opportunity to learn from their heavenly Father through instruction and example. We can see in the story that after the disobedience of Adam and Eve God personally came to visit and communicate with them. This was the relationship God wanted to have with them, and it is the relationship He wants to have with us.

Knowledge is something we can obtain quickly. When we have knowledge, we often become puffed up to believe we have all the information; hence, we can make our own decisions. The Scriptures warn of the danger of knowledge puffing us up with pride causing us to not make the right decisions.

> *Now concerning things offered to idols: We know that we all have knowledge. Knowledge puffs up, but love edifies.* (1 Corinthians 8:1)

When Eve gained knowledge from the serpent, it made her usurp God's authority and guidance and make a decision on her own. It was a decision neither she nor Adam were capable of making. This is the story of youth and why God gives leadership to help guide us. Although God was guiding man, He was not controlling man nor does He control us. His plan is to allow room for choice and failure thus providing us the opportunity to grow in maturity. This is a real danger in our modern times when knowledge is increasing at such a fast rate. Our knowledge could puff us up giving us an opportunity for extreme foolishness, or we could understand the need to temper our knowledge with character and structure so our knowledge does not become our ruin.

Most people have accepted the need for knowledge. Education and knowledge have been given an esteemed place in modern society. Many parents will go to great lengths to be sure their children are given the advantage of an advanced education, but they have failed to understand the vital place of parenting and leadership.

This is why the Bible endorses the concept of eldership. A certain level of instruction can only come from the elders. This is why in our modern age of affluence and opportunities we cannot disengage from the purpose of God when we get older. Many people think the golden years are the time to think about themselves and retire to a life of leisure. The church and the family need the leadership of elders. This principle has always been recognized by societies. However, the modern era has placed more value on the youth. In this fast changing, technological age, the need for quick and innovative thinking has become valuable. These traits are typically more common in the youth. However, history has proven whenever we fail to learn from the past we will repeat the mistakes of the past. With this in mind, we should see how important it is to view those who have lived in the past as very essential to the purpose God has for His people.

Adam and Eve, no doubt, were created with potential beyond what we could imagine, but they needed to be under the oversight of God with His instructions and commands until the appointed time. The serpent beguiled Eve into thinking she would be able to make her own decisions without God, but she and her husband were simply victims of their own desires. They missed the timing of God.

This is just like when we raise children. They think parenting is the act of denying them the fun they could so easily have if they were without oversight. I remember as a kid thinking how wonderful it would be to be the parent and to be in charge. Do what you want to do, when you want to, is what it looks like to a child. I remember looking forward to each birthday with anticipation because the older you got the more freedom life offered. When you're a kid, when someone asks your age, you always round it off to the next highest number. That will certainly change when you get older! You also see growing older as the opportunity to experience more of life: driving a car, getting married, or getting a job so you can have your own money. Unfortunately, we often fail to think about the responsibility of those opportunities. I also remember growing up thinking how great it would be to be a parent so I could do my own thing. Parents seemed to have all the freedom; but as kids, we just had to do what we were told. Nobody was telling the parents what to do. They just did what they wanted.

Of course that wasn't true. The reason we had a house and provisions for life was because my father worked, and we had a nice home because my mother made it so. Nobody told them what to do; they just fulfilled their responsibilities as parents. They had personal and recreational time, but all that had to revolve around their responsibilities and work. Life in many ways was ordered for them because they chose the route of being responsible parents.

I grew up in a family of nine children. Having a large family required a hierarchy in order to help facilitate all the needs which could not be fully handled by my parents. The older children were given responsibilities to help with the family. The oldest child would watch the kids and the house when the parents were away. Since the process of time meant the oldest was also leaving to go into adulthood or jobs of their own, the "babysitter" would change over time. I remember when my time arrived. After my parents left, I snapped my belt and announced who was in charge and what the rules would be. At 9:00 everyone would go to bed, and I would be up as an adult in charge of my world. I could watch what I wanted on television and eat what I wanted in the kitchen. I would go to bed when I was ready because I was in charge now. All went well until I became afraid being up by myself, and I informed my younger sister that I thought she was old enough so I would let her get up too!

Every freedom sounds good until you realize freedom comes with responsibilities, and you must be mature enough to handle them. For many people, the New Testament ushered in the time of grace. For them grace, being God's "unmerited" favor, meant Jesus Christ died so we could do what we wanted to do without consequences. We think that way only because we are immature. As children, we want freedom without responsibility. Did Jesus Christ die on the cross so you wouldn't have to be responsible for your actions? People who teach "original sin" and "total depravity" would have us believe the purpose of the law was simply to show us how despicable we are. It came so we could see there was no good thing in us. After all, who could keep the law of God? When Jesus Christ came, was it true that the Pharisees could not keep the law or was their problem they did not have a heart for God? The obvious answer was they could indeed clean up the outside of the vessel; it was the inside they had problems with.

> *Woe to you, scribes and Pharisees, hypocrites! For you are like whitewashed tombs which indeed appear beautiful outwardly, but inside are full of dead men's bones and all uncleanness. Even so you also outwardly appear righteous to men, but inside you are full of hypocrisy and lawlessness.* (Matthew 23:27-28)

The failure of the law is that it could not change a person's heart. In a human family, if a child could only see the rules of the house as bondage they could grow up as adults simply wanting to rebel against their upbringing. The only way they would learn was

135

when they saw the wisdom of the rules and the proper motivation of those who had trained them. This is why man rebelled in the garden. The serpent beguiled Eve into seeing God as someone self centered who only wanted to control her for His own purpose. Many of God's people see God the same way. They don't rebel on the outside like Eve, but it really is what they believe, so they try to be the best slaves they can in order to earn the favor of the controlling God. That is what happened in the garden. In the end, they found out what it was like to be on their own, unprotected, and having to make their own provision. They found out they should have waited on the timing of God.

One of the greatest lies propagated by the enemy in the garden that is still believed today is that God is a controlling God. In evangelical churches, we are taught to be obedient. In charismatic and Pentecostal services, we think the Holy Spirit wants to take control. I have news for you, demons want to control you; God wants to guide you!

If God were controlling, would He have given man a choice in the garden? God didn't have to give them a choice. He could have given them a choice without any information, and they would have been obedient just out of ignorance. Instead, God gave them an advocate for the opposite opinion. God is always putting choices before us.

My experience as a pastor for thirty-three years tells me most people don't really want to make choices. That is why people simply want to follow the crowd. Why don't people want choices? We really don't want to accept responsibility for our choices. That's why we have made grace into something different than what God intended it to be. Grace often becomes another way to avoid responsibility.

This concept not only holds true for us as individuals but for mankind as a whole. We need to see history as man developing over time with our Father's oversight. God holds everything in His hands but lets history unfold with man learning and developing over time. As mankind has grown, we have increased in our capacity to fulfill the plan and purpose of God. This is quite contrary to many who

136

only see man as an "inferior" product who is simply reliving history and proving his own lack of worth. This is why we have always looked with apprehension to the future. We thought all history could do is prove our poor makeup. This is so contrary to what God says about Himself. The Word declares that He will finish what He has started.

> *being confident of this very thing, that He who has begun a good work in you will complete it until the day of Jesus Christ;* (Philippians 1:6)

This concept is aptly demonstrated in the dealings of God with the house of Israel. When Jesus Christ came to the world, He came to inaugurate a new era for the people of God. He was very specific. He came to the lost sheep of the house of Israel. He came to bring about a change that God said they should be ready to make. He wanted them to quit being little children and to become more fully His sons. In the Old Testament, He dealt with them as children. Now, they would not be children in the way God would deal with them.

We put our children under laws and closely monitor their behavior to protect them from themselves. When the time comes, we release them to live their lives. Our thinking is that they will not abandon what we have taught them and that they will respond from our instruction by doing what is right in fulfilling their own destiny. You treat children as servants when they are young with the idea they will grow and develop into heirs of the family assets with personal accomplishments. They will hopefully excel and make you proud. This is how the Word describes the transition from the old covenant to the new covenant.

> *Now I say that the heir, as long as he is a child, does not differ at all from a slave, though he is master of all, but is under guardians and stewards until the time appointed by the father. Even so we, when we were children, were in bondage under the elements of the world. But when the fullness of the*

time had come, God sent forth His Son, born of a woman, born under the law, to redeem those who were under the law, that we might receive the adoption as sons. (Galatians 4:1-5)

The Scriptures use the term "children of Israel" over 600 times. Their identity was in their natural lineage. God wanted them to have the identity as His children. They could not have this identity as long as they were only born according to the flesh. In the new covenant, they would have the ability to be born of the Spirit of God through faith in Jesus Christ. When this happened, they would no longer have an earthly identity but would lose that to take on a new identity as the promised seed of Abraham.

For you are all sons of God through faith in Christ Jesus. For as many of you as were baptized into Christ have put on Christ. There is neither Jew nor Greek, there is neither slave nor free, there is neither male nor female; for you are all one in Christ Jesus. And if you are Christ's, then you are Abraham's seed, and heirs according to the promise. (Galatians 3:26-29)

In the Old Testament, only the angels were referred to as the sons of God. Yet, Jesus Christ spoke of the sons of the resurrection who would, like the angels, be the sons of God.

But those who are counted worthy to attain that age, and the resurrection from the dead, neither marry nor are given in marriage; nor can they die anymore, for they are equal to the angels and are sons of God, being sons of the resurrection. (Luke 20:35-36)

The Scriptures also speak of the people on the earth who are called the sons of God. These are the ones who have learned to be led by the Spirit of God.

For as many as are led by the Spirit of God, these are sons of God. For you did not receive the spirit of bondage again to fear, but you received the Spirit of adoption by whom we cry out, "Abba, Father." The Spirit Himself bears witness with our spirit that we are children of God, and if children, then heirs — heirs of God and joint heirs with Christ, if indeed we suffer with Him, that we may also be glorified together. (Romans 8:14-17)

When we are born again, we become the children of God. But when we grow in the things of the spirit, we become the sons of God in the earth taking on the image of Jesus Christ. This is when we qualify for our inheritance with Christ and when we will reveal the glory of God in the earth. This is why the whole of creation looks for us to grow into the place God has divinely chosen for us since before the foundation of the world.

For the earnest expectation of the creation eagerly waits for the revealing of the sons of God. For the creation was subjected to futility, not willingly, but because of Him who subjected it in hope; because the creation itself also will be delivered from the bondage of corruption into the glorious liberty of the children of God. (Romans 8:19-21)

The concept of the sons of God is a concept only possible in the New Testament. Although the children of Israel were born as children of promise through the faith of Abraham, they were still fleshly in personal behavior because they were indeed children of the flesh. As the natural seed of Abraham, they are heirs of the natural promise. The natural promise God gave to Abraham was limited to a small piece of real estate in the Middle East. This inheritance was reserved for His seed according to the flesh; but for those who are children of the promise, this inheritance was for the whole world, not just a portion.

For the promise that he would be the heir of the world was not to Abraham or to his seed through the law, but through the righteousness of faith. For if those who are of the law are heirs, faith is made void and the promise made of no effect, (Romans 4:13-14)

What is the difference between the two covenants? One covenant is of the flesh and the other is of faith through the promise. What is the difference between the children of Israel and the sons of God? The children still live motivated by their fleshly desires, but those who become the sons of God will be those who fulfill their Father's desire like Jesus Christ. Life comes through Christ and by living according to the Spirit of God.

> *For those who live according to the flesh set their minds on the things of the flesh, but those who live according to the Spirit, the things of the Spirit. For to be carnally minded is death, but to be spiritually minded is life and peace. Because the carnal mind is enmity against God; for it is not subject to the law of God, nor indeed can be. So then, those who are in the flesh cannot please God.* (Romans 8:5-8)

This was the condition of man in the garden of Eden. Although they were created to become the sons of God with dominion, they were just children ultimately succumbing to their fleshly desires. This is no different than children in the natural order who really come into the world craving for the satisfaction of their physical and emotional comfort; and when this comfort is not available to them, they cry out for satisfaction. As parents, we scurry to meet their needs and find great satisfaction in the sense of love we get from them in return. Yet as they mature, we learn to sort out their needs from their selfish desires. If we are good parents, we will carefully make them understand that the world does not revolve around them; and they must come to the place of maturity where they become contributing citizens and family members. This process will lead to a maturity that will give them the capacity to become parents and repeat the cycle. This is God's desire for us. He desires us to be no more children but to grow into the image and stature of Christ.

And He Himself gave some to be apostles, some prophets, some evangelists, and some pastors and teachers, for the equipping of the saints for the work of ministry, for the edifying of the body of Christ, till we all come to the unity of the faith and of the knowledge of the Son of God, to a perfect man, to the measure of the stature of the fullness of Christ; that we should no longer be children, tossed to and fro and carried about with every wind of doctrine, by the trickery of men, in the cunning craftiness of deceitful plotting, but, speaking the truth in love, may grow up in all things into Him who is the head — Christ — from whom the whole body, joined and knit together by what every joint supplies, according to the effective working by which every part does its share, causes growth of the body for the edifying of itself in love. (Ephesians 4:11-16)

The children of Israel never attained this place. Although they suffered for their disobedience, this was the only lesson they learned. Obedience is the lesson of a child. When a person is mature, it is no longer an issue of obedience but an issue of responsibility. Most of God's children live in the obedience realm, when the Father is looking for us to grow past that stage. Our inheritance will not just come because we are obedient. It will come because we can be trusted with responsibility. As adults in the natural order, we may still have "issues." The problem is not whether you have issues, but will you be willing to step out of the center of your world and give yourself to the responsibility of the eternal purpose the Father has for you? Are you going to be a child in your Father's house, or will you be a son in the Father's business? The Father's business is His kingdom, and He is calling us now to take the place of authority and blessing He has for us as full heir sons of God!

In Summary

Many people believe that the ability to discern good and evil is the result of the choice of Adam and Eve in the garden of Eden. The issue for God was not that we would have the ability to discern good and evil, but when and how this ability would come about. God's plan has a timetable and a pattern. Our mistakes will impact our lives but will never change God's plan.

God's original plan was for man to take dominion as His sons in the earth when we are ready for the responsibility He has for us. Just like in the natural, we start as children and when we are ready God gives us an opportunity to grow up and take dominion. Adam and Eve were created as adults and they required much training and development before they could have been fully given the charge God had for them. God did not intend for them to remain in a state of innocence forever. He wanted to equip them for a place of authority, so that when they were given dominion they could take responsibility for it. In the garden, they were given time to learn and grow. Through their choice to take control of their own life, they stepped out of the timing of God.

Knowledge, when we are not ready for it, can be our ruin. We need to temper our knowledge with character and structure. Knowledge should include responsibility. Leadership is important. With good leadership, we can learn through examples so that we can be spared mistakes. When we do make mistakes, we have the grace of God which empowers us to get through the consequences and to get back on the path God intended for us. We must see the wisdom of rules. We must see God not as a God who wants to control us but a God who wants to guide us. God has given us choices. Would He do that if He wanted to control us?

Chapter Ten

How Can Love Be the Destiny?

There is no fear in love; but perfect love casts out fear, because fear involves torment. But he who fears has not been made perfect in love. We love Him because He first loved us. (1 John 4:18-19)

Once we understand the change from the Old Testament to the New Testament, we can fully understand the concepts of grace and love. In order to understand the work of grace and love in our life, we must understand its relationship to the law. What was the purpose of the law? It was to bring us to the time of maturity when we could be released from the structures of childhood to become mature sons of God. The main aspect of this maturity process requires us to grow in grace and love. As we grow in grace, we understand it is not just a pass from responsibility but God's opportunity for empowerment that allows us to grow into our complete destiny. Certainly, if we truly love God, we would desire to live a life pleasing to Him. This is why Jesus Christ made it very clear He did not come to do away with the law.

Do not think that I came to destroy the Law or the Prophets. I did not come to destroy but to fulfill. For assuredly, I say to you, till heaven and earth pass away, one jot or one tittle will by no means pass from the law till all is fulfilled. (Matthew 5:17-18)

Not only did Jesus not do away with the law, He in a sense enlarged it. The laws of the Old Testament were given as a structure for the true believer whose heart was in line with God's. Jesus said we should not think of the laws from their individual application, but we should use them as a way to see the greater picture. God wants to have our heart, mind, and soul. Then He wants us to make every choice and action based upon the perimeter of His love.

> *Jesus said to him, "'You shall love the LORD your God with all your heart, with all your soul, and with all your mind.' This is the first and great commandment. And the second is like it: 'You shall love your neighbor as yourself.' On these two commandments hang all the Law and the Prophets."* (Matthew 22:37-40)

Since this sums up all the law, we realize when we were children under the law, God wanted to teach us how to love. Once you take away the body of the law and replace it with the heart of God, it becomes a broader commandment, not a narrower one. When someone gives me a law, I can work my way around it; or I can follow it without fully engaging my heart. Without the specifics of the instruction, the law of spirit requires my constant vigilance to the command. This was demonstrated when someone tried to put the golden rule to use as something from the letter of the law, rather than something of the spirit. The story, of course, involves a lawyer who asks Jesus a question about this rule.

> *But he, wanting to justify himself, said to Jesus, "And who is my neighbor?"* (Luke 10:29)

The legalistic approach will always beg the question of the extent of the commandment. In the parable of the Good Samaritan, Jesus tells about a person who is the victim of a violent crime, tossed on the side of the road, and in need of assistance. In this story, both a priest and a Levite, those separated for the work of the ministry, passed by the hurting man ignoring the man and his problem. A Samaritan, someone despised by the Jews, stopped and cared for the man ministering to his needs. Jesus then asked the question, "Who was a neighbor to the victim?" When the law of commandment is replaced by the law of the heart, the issue becomes reflective upon the heart of the person, rather than an issue of what is happening around him. This is the difference between the Old and New Testaments, and this is the difference between an immature person and a mature one.

It is interesting how most people think the new covenant is less demanding than the old covenant. The fact is God has always been looking for us to give Him our heart. When God has our heart, He has our whole being. This is not a control issue but a motivation issue. What motivates our response will not just determine our actions but our attitudes. God's demands have never been unreasonable but very reasonable. It is still reasonable for God to expect us to give ourselves fully to Him in this new covenant of grace. This giving of oneself will result in a change of mind that will fulfill the perfect or mature will God wants us to walk in.

> *I beseech you therefore, brethren, by the mercies of God, that you present your bodies a living sacrifice, holy, acceptable to God, which is your reasonable service. And do not be conformed to this world, but be transformed by the renewing of your mind, that you may prove what is that good and acceptable and perfect will of God.* (Romans 12:1-2)

Interestingly enough, many people want to throw off the shackles of legalism but approach the effort through a legalistic mindset. Often the first approach, is to have fewer laws or less stringent laws; yet, they still have the mindset of a legalist. Others will say, "I am under grace." Although they do not feel bound to those laws because of God's mercy, they still see themselves relating to God from a legalistic frame of thinking. God wants to reorder our whole process of thinking by taking our walk with God to a deeper level. This level consists of a heart relationship with God based upon love.

Over the years, trying to arbitrate marital crises, I have found people want to counsel on a legalistic basis. The idea is that if I can get the other person to do what I want or fulfill my desires I will be happy, and I will have a good marriage. These people have certainly forgotten the time of love when their pursuit was to contemplate ahead of time what would please the other person. You don't want them to have to ask; you want to show them your knowledge of them and your desire to please them. This is the basis of a true love relationship.

The first step in rebuilding a relationship is to get the love back. This is why the apostle John in Revelations, enjoined the church of Ephesus to return to their first love or risk losing the candlestick of His presence from their midst. We all want love. It is literally a part of our makeup. You were created in the image and likeness of God. God is love! Remember, God doesn't just love; it is the essence of His person. This is why the pursuit of love is a normal part of our human quest. Unfortunately, unless we see love as it is defined through God, our love will be imperfect and not satisfying.

God demonstrates to us the way to get love is to give it. If you're looking for love, you need to give up your search and draw from your own resources. As you begin to give it out, it will start coming back to you. Everything about God's eternal plan for man starts with Him choosing us. This choice was not based on your actions. The Bible is clear. God loved you before any action of yours could be taken to mean His love was in response to your actions.

> *And not only this, but when Rebecca also had conceived by one man, even by our father Isaac (for the children not yet being born, nor having done any good or evil, that the purpose of God according to election might stand, not of works but of Him who calls), it was said to her, "The older shall serve the younger." As it is written, "Jacob I have loved, but Esau I have hated." (Romans 9:10-13)*

This may seem like an uncomfortable concept; but if someone says they love everybody, I don't think they know what love is. If you love someone, this means you think and feel more about them than you do someone else. If you tell me you love me and follow that up with the statement that "you love everybody," then I would think your love was not real or certainly not special.

The Scripture says, *"for God so loved the world that He gave His only begotten Son."* For God to love the world means He loves His creation and His plan for the world. It says He loves people because they are the crowning glory of His purpose, but it does not say God loves everybody. God's love is for His people. He loved you first; that is why you are reading this book and seeking after God. The question now is will you love Him back in response to His love, or will you serve Him as a slave so you can get the rewards of your labor?

As I mentioned earlier in this book, a lot of the concepts we develop are to explain uncomfortable principles in the Word of God or things we can't easily explain. Our thought is likely to be: What about the people God doesn't love? I propose we hear what Jesus said to the apostle Peter when He wanted to question what God was doing in someone else's life.

> *Then Peter, turning around, saw the disciple whom Jesus loved following, who also had leaned on His breast at the supper, and said, "Lord, who is the one who betrays You?" Peter, seeing him, said to Jesus, "But Lord, what about this man?" Jesus said to him, "If I will that he remain till I come, what is that to you? You follow Me." Then this saying went out among the brethren that this disciple would not die. Yet Jesus did not say to him that he would not die, but, "If I will that he remain till I come, what is that to you?"* (John 21:20-23)

The Word of God is a revelation of God and His people. Leave the things we don't know to the Almighty, trusting in Him, and deal with the truth as it pertains to us.

147

The Scripture is very clear that God's ways are not our ways, nor are His thoughts ours. We need to leave the things that are above us in the hands of God and see ourselves in His hand! One important lesson God wanted His people in the old covenant to know was that they were a "special people." Because they did not see themselves as special, they were always trying to be like everybody else. When they were leaving Egypt, they were always looking back to the "good old days" back in Egypt. God wanted them to see how special they were, and all they could do was think about Egypt. As slaves, they were constantly reminded of their inferiority to their Egyptian masters. This unconscious voice on the inside was a reproach they could not carry into the Promised Land.

> *Then Joshua circumcised their sons whom He raised up in their place; for they were uncircumcised, because they had not been circumcised on the way. So it was, when they had finished circumcising all the people, that they stayed in their places in the camp till they were healed. Then the LORD said to Joshua, "This day I have rolled away the reproach of Egypt from you." Therefore the name of the place is called Gilgal to this day.* (Joshua 5:7-9)

The word "reproach" here means to "carp at, harp upon, or to pull off." The children of Israel were robbed of their sense of specialness by the criticism of their captors. As a result, they had abandoned their identity by failing to observe the rite of circumcision. Through circumcision, the outward problem would be cured; but the heart condition did not change because they failed to allow their minds and hearts to change.

The concept of being special is still a part of God's plan for His people.

> *But you are a chosen generation, a royal priesthood, a holy nation, His own special people, that you may proclaim the praises of Him who called you out of darkness into His marvelous light; who once were not a people but are now the peo-*

ple of God, who had not obtained mercy but now have obtained mercy. (1 Peter 2:9-10)

You are special because God has set His love upon you. God setting His love upon us makes us a special people. As His special people, He has provided an avenue into the holy place of His presence. It is a place we could not approach without the provision of the sacrifice of the blood of Jesus Christ.

Why did Jesus have to offer His blood for our sins? We know that the purpose of the blood was for the remission or cleansing of our sin. This purging was not so we could get away from the demands of God but so we could pursue God and come into His presence with boldness and confidence. Besides the laws of God in the old covenant, there were also the ordinances that had to do with their religious rituals. The tabernacle displayed the order of entering into the presence of God. Starting at the outer court, the progression into the presence of God went into the third level of the Most Holy Place. This level could only be open to the high priest who once a year came to provide the sacrificial offering for the sins of the nation on the Day of Atonement. When Jesus Christ offered His blood once and for all on the heavenly mercy seat, the way to God was fully opened to us. His blood offered was love making the way for us. It was God opening Himself to us and saying, "Come to me; I want to have a love relationship with you."

Just as God wants a special love relationship with us, we should desire one with Him. God wants to be "special" to His people. This is why I like the concept that God is a jealous God. Some people find this to be an unpleasant attribute, but it tells me God loves me enough to care about my response to Him. He desires reciprocal love. He wants us to love Him with the same willingness to sacrifice for Him as He has sacrificed for us. When you love someone, you are jealous for their attention. You want to know you are getting the attention and effort love requires. How could you say you love someone and not want to get your share of their life? This is true of God. Keep in mind; God is not covetous. He doesn't want all of us; He only wants an attitude of giving all to Him. If God were covetous, He would have told Adam, when He observed it wasn't good for him to be alone, to suck it up and get more satisfaction from Him. Instead, God created a woman for him, which was a compliment to an already generous provision in the garden of Eden. What a generous and loving God we have!

Once we have responded to God's offer of a loving relationship with Him, we need to go into His presence fully confident He has paved the way for us. Yet as we go forth in this love, we shouldn't go as little children only thinking about our own needs and desires. God doesn't just think of Himself; He thinks of us, and we should go forward as responsible lovers willing to do the same. We should go forward offering to God what He has offered to us, giving ourselves fully to Him in love as He has given Himself to us! Love cannot be defined from the human experience but from God who is love. How does God describe true love?

> *Love suffers long and is kind; love does not envy; love does not parade itself, is not puffed up; does not behave rudely, does not seek its own, is not provoked, thinks no evil; does not rejoice in iniquity, but rejoices in the truth; bears all things, believes all things, hopes all things, endures all things. Love never fails.* (1 Corinthians 13:4-8)

The part that says, *does not seek its own*, is the centerpiece of the whole description. Love is not about you. Love motivates you to live above you! Isn't this the true lesson of the natural order of the family? When we come into the world, everything is about us and our needs. To us, love is about someone responding to our needs and taking care of us. As we grow, the responsibility of our parents is to not only care for us but to teach us to grow and accept responsibility for our own needs. This is not the end of the matter however. The growth to maturity is to bring us to the place of meeting the needs of others. Marriage was instituted by God to help us in life but also puts us in a relationship where the other person needs what we have to offer. When we become adults, we start looking for love in a lifetime companion. When you find that person and become married, you should realize the relationship is not about you but about the other person. Marriage is difficult because it requires you to step out of yourself, meet the needs of another person, and adjust to a person who is usually quite opposite of you. Your motivation is a natural and God given motivation. Working out your relationship is not natural; it takes something supernatural to make it work proficiently. This is why marriage is not just about two people. It is a relationship that needs divine help. If you let God's Word guide you and His spirit help you, you will grow in life and in love. This is why marriage needs to be a covenant commitment. It needs a commitment and God.

> *Again, if two lie down together, they will keep warm; But how can one be warm alone? Though one may be overpowered by another, two can withstand him. And a threefold cord is not quickly broken.* (Ecclesiastes 4:11-12)

After people get married, there typically comes another natural progression, children. Children and the intimate relationship that conceives them is easy and natural; raising children is another story. If you are to be a good parent, you need to follow God's Word and seek His help because children take us out of our self focused life to a life focused on someone else. This is when love has its consummation in the natural life. This is the pattern God wants us to give ourselves to in order to truly grow in His love. Our spiritual life should also follow this pattern in the house of God. As you grow in God, the church should not just be about what it offers you. It should also be about what it requires of you so you can grow in love and so the house of God can be a place where the Father can produce children. The church should bring those children to maturity as full heir sons. Our mindset about the eternal plan of God needs to change. We must change how we function in the house of God so the eternal plan of God can be consummated in the earth.

When we are born again, we become as children in order to enter the kingdom of God. Since the church is a place for children, we need to be very mindful of how we treat each other, especially those who are new to God's house. Yet, it is very important to realize the conflicts of the church are no different than the conflicts in the family. When offenses come, we need to see them as our opportunity to grow in the Lord.

> *Then Jesus called a little child to Him, set him in the midst of them, and said, "Assuredly, I say to you, unless you are converted and become as little children, you will by no means enter the kingdom of heaven. Therefore whoever humbles himself as this little child is the greatest in the kingdom of heaven. Whoever receives one little child like this in My name receives Me. Whoever causes one of these little ones who believe in Me to sin, it would be better for him if a millstone were hung around his neck, and he were drowned in the depth of the sea. Woe to the world because of offenses! For offenses must come, but woe to that man by whom the offense comes! (Matthew 18:2-7)*

Our motivation in love is not to create offenses; however, we must realize offenses will come. How we deal with offense will determine our ability to grow in the Lord. Many people go through life never dealing with the issues of their upbringing. These people often are hindered in their ability to fully have loving relationships with others or create a good environment for a healthy family. The family is the foundation God has given for our proper development. This is why the house of God, the church, becomes integral in perfecting love in the people of God. The house of God gives us the opportunity to grow in the ways we did not grow in our natural family. It is time for us to see the house of God as the place for this plan to be fulfilled and to see why the church is an integral part of God's eternal plan. Be careful you are not isolated because of the past, but allow God to place you in His family; and let the family become your source to grow in the love of God.

Matthew 18, talks about how to deal with offenses on a mature level. If someone has an offense they cannot deal with personally, then they should bring the offense to the church. The church should be a place of judgment in order to purge out the things that will be detrimental to the house.

> *Do you not know that the saints will judge the world? And if the world will be judged by you, are you unworthy to judge the smallest matters? Do you not know that we shall judge angels? How much more, things that pertain to this life?* (1 Corinthians 6:2-3)

The authority of the church should be so honored that the people who refuse to listen are considered sinners and not saints.

> *But if he will not hear, take with you one or two more, that 'by the mouth of two or three witnesses every word may be established.' And if he refuses to hear them, tell it to the church. But if he refuses even to hear the church, let him be to you like a heathen and a tax collector.* (Matthew 18:16-17)

This authority is necessary to protect the church from predators who want to feast on the people of God. But we must be very careful not to forget the end result of our endeavor. The purpose of this process is to provide an opportunity for love to grow. Our end goal should not be personal justification or making sure we are considered the person in the right. If love is our motivation, then reconciliation and harmony in the body must be our aim. Jesus follows up this discourse by teaching the importance of love and forgiveness.

> *Then Peter came to Him and said, "Lord, how often shall my brother sin against me, and I forgive him? Up to seven times?" Jesus said to him, "I do not say to you, up to seven times, but up to seventy times seven.* (Matthew 18:21-22)

The goal of the legalist will always be to prove they are right. The goal of the person under grace is to bring reconciliation.

Jesus goes on to tell the story of forgiveness. He tells about a person heavily in debt. Because he was unable to pay his debt, his master proposed he and his family would be sold into slavery. This would have been a customary penalty that would provide the offended party the funds they were owed. The servant fell down and begged for mercy. The master was moved with compassion, released him, and forgave his debt. This same servant was owed money by another of the servants. He grabbed the person by the throat and demanded payment. When his fellow servants reported this to the master, he changed his mind about the debt owed him and had the wicked servant turned over to the torturers. Those of us who have received the loving mercy and forgiveness of God are expected to walk in this same spirit. As we work through our conflicts, we need to allow God to work His love in and through us.

This perfected love has a twofold reality. As we pay the cost to give out this love, we will begin to see the cost of God's love given to us. This understanding of love will dispel any fear we have of God and give us the boldness to move forward into His presence. Moving forward in His presence will also cause us to confidently move forward in our eternal purpose. Like the child raised in a loving family, we will be able to establish our adult identity and continue the cycle of the generations.

One day I sat in my office with a person much older than myself and he said, "All I want to know is that my father loves me." He had been through a difficult childhood. In the experience of life, he had not really received the proper love. This made the person incapable of love and still longing for the past. My children, at this time in life, were very young. When I went home, I told my wife that if we want our children to long for us forever then we have to start being bad parents. If we do, when they get old they will go everywhere telling people how much they long for us!

It was only a joke, of course, but I have found that people who are not loved always long for love and become incapable of giving it. It is the same in God's house. If we fail to relate to our Father's love, we will never be able to truly love; and fear will destroy our relationships every time. If we truly learn, through the process of life, the love God has for us, we will be able to not only love God but our fellow man. Some people can mask their fear of God's love, but the evidence is in our lack of love for our fellowman. Since God is invisible, we can make up our spiritual experiences; but in our relationships with people we have to face the reality of how to love. It is clear from the Scripture that our human relationships are the sign of our spiritual one.

> *If someone says, "I love God," and hates his brother, he is a liar; for he who does not love his brother whom he has seen, how can he love God whom he has not seen? And this commandment we have from Him: that he who loves God must love his brother also.* (1 John 4:20-21)

It is time for us to grow into the fullness of God's love. This love surpasses our human understanding because it does not always respond in the natural way. This is why we need to grow into the revelation and experience of this love. When we do, we will also be filled with all the fullness of God!

> *For this reason I bow my knees to the Father of our Lord Jesus Christ, from whom the whole family in heaven and earth is named, that He would grant you, according to the riches of His glory, to be strengthened with might through His Spirit in the inner man, that Christ may dwell in your hearts through faith; that you, being rooted and grounded in love, may be able to comprehend with all the saints what is the width and length and depth and height — to know the love of Christ which passes knowledge; that you may be filled with all the fullness of God.* (Ephesians 3:14-19)

In Summary

In order to understand the work of grace and love in our life, we must understand its relationship to the law. What was the purpose of the law? It was to bring us to the time of maturity when we could be released from the structures of childhood to become mature sons of God. As we grow in grace, we understand it is not just a pass from responsibility but God's opportunity for empowerment that allows us to grow into our complete destiny. In this way, love becomes our destiny. Jesus Christ made it very clear He did not come to do away with the law but to enlarge it. Once you take away the body of the law and replace it with the heart of God, it becomes a broader commandment, not a narrower one. God is looking for us to give Him our heart. Our love for Him becomes our motivation. God wants our relationship with Him to be based on our desire to contemplate ahead of time what He desires from us and to follow through with our actions. God is love. We were created in His image and likeness. Love can only be defined through God. God loved you first. The question now is will you love Him back in response to His love, or will you serve Him as a slave so you can get the rewards of your labor?

You are special because God has set His love upon you. As His special people, He has provided an avenue into the holy place of His presence. It is a place we could not approach without the provision of the sacrifice of the blood of Jesus Christ as the remission or cleansing for our sin. This purging was not so we could get away from the demands of God but so we could pursue God and come into His presence with boldness and confidence. His blood offered was love making the way for us. He desires reciprocal love. He wants us to love Him with the same willingness to sacrifice for Him as He has sacrificed for us. Love is not about you. Love motivates you to live above you! The growth to maturity is to bring us to the place of meeting the needs of others.

This understanding of love should operate in the church. The church should not just be about what it offers you. It should also be about what it requires of you, so you can grow in love, and so the house of God can be a place where the Father can produce children. When offenses come, as they will, we need to see them as our opportunity to grow in the Lord. How we deal with offense will determine our ability to grow in the Lord. If love is our motivation, then reconciliation and harmony in the body must be our aim. The goal of the legalist will always be to prove they are right. The goal of the person under grace is to bring reconciliation. If we fail to relate to our Father's love, we will never be able to truly love. If we truly learn, through the process of life, the love God has for us, we will be able to not only love God but our fellow man.

Chapter Eleven

WHAT IS THE SIGN OF THE "END OF TIME"?

Therefore be patient, brethren, until the coming of the Lord. See how the farmer waits for the precious fruit of the earth, waiting patiently for it until it receives the early and latter rain. You also be patient. Establish your hearts, for the coming of the Lord is at hand. (James 5:7-8)

Since the earliest days of the Christian church, we have waited with expectation for the "blessed hope" of the return of our Savior, Jesus Christ. When He left on a cloud, He said He would return in like manner. What a wonderful thought to see the heavens opened and to witness our Lord's return. Unfortunately, our expectation has often influenced our thinking to look for His return before the appointed time of God. When Jesus Christ spoke of His return, His disciples wanted to know the signs of His return and perhaps a specific time. Jesus Christ made it very clear the appointed time was only known by the Father and not even by Him as the Son of God.

But of that day and hour no one knows, not even the angels in heaven, nor the Son, but only the Father. Take heed, watch and pray; for you do not know when the time is. (Mark 13:32-33)

Growing up in church, I often heard sermons on the signs of the coming of Jesus Christ. Most of them are gleaned from the discourse of Matthew 24. What is often overlooked is that Jesus Christ is talking more about the impending judgment of Jerusalem and the destruction of the temple than about His return. Remember, although Jesus Christ told of His death, burial, and resurrection the disciples were too dull in their understanding to fully comprehend what He was saying. Jesus Christ did say something very important about discerning the appointed times of God. He told them the best way to discern the time was to watch for fruit.

> *Now learn this parable from the fig tree: When its branch has already become tender and puts forth leaves, you know that summer is near. So you also, when you see all these things, know that it is near — at the doors!* (Matthew 24:32-33)

Many of the things Jesus Christ spoke of: wars, tribulations, and natural disasters are common to every age. But if you are looking for the fruit of the time, it is a more recognizable thing. This is especially true if you are looking for the same fruit God is. We know the farmer, or husbandman of the earth, has long patience in His plan and purpose. He has appointed times for the rains to come and times for the full harvest. We need to be apprised of what God is looking for and be looking for the same things. Often when thinking about the end of time, people are more likely to be looking for the negative rather than the positive fruit of the earth. We must recognize there are two harvests in the earth: one that pertains to God's plan and the other that is the result of the fruit of man's labor. The works of the flesh have produced the vine of the earth. The vine of the earth will produce fruit that will lead to the judgment of God.

> *And another angel came out from the altar, who had power over fire, and he cried with a loud cry to him who had the sharp sickle, saying, "Thrust in your sharp sickle and gather the clusters of the vine of the earth, for her grapes are fully ripe." So the angel thrust his sickle into the earth and gath-*

ered the vine of the earth, and threw it into the great wine-press of the wrath of God. (Revelation 14:18-19)

The other vine is the vine of Christ. This vine will produce the glory of the Lord. It is this vine that is most indicative of the end of time. It is only when the Father has His fruit that the end will come. The book of James is very clear that the farmer of the earth has patience for the fruit of the earth. We must also understand God, as the farmer or vinedresser of the earth, is also diligent in His efforts to produce the fruit He is looking for.

I am the true vine, and My Father is the vinedresser. Every branch in Me that does not bear fruit He takes away; and every branch that bears fruit He prunes, that it may bear more fruit. You are already clean because of the word which I have spoken to you. Abide in Me, and I in you. As the branch cannot bear fruit of itself, unless it abides in the vine, neither can you, unless you abide in Me. (John 15:1-4)

These Scriptures make it very clear God has a purpose for bringing forth fruit from His people, and He meticulously observes and develops the fruit produced from us. When God comes to make an inspection, we call it a day of visitation. When God comes to visit, we need to understand He comes looking for something. We shouldn't always be looking for what God is bringing us, but our desire should be when He comes He sees we have prepared something for Him. This is why churches have foolishly looked for the coming of the Lord without understanding the responsibility that comes with it. The prophets of old declared this to the people of God.

In all vineyards there shall be wailing, For I will pass through you," Says the LORD. Woe to you who desire the day of the LORD! For what good is the day of the LORD to you? It will be darkness, and not light. It will be as though a man fled from a lion, And a bear met him! Or as though he went into

161

the house, Leaned his hand on the wall, And a serpent bit him! (Amos 5:17 -19)

When God is passing through His vineyards, He is looking for fruit. Unfortunately, we look forward to the coming of the Lord to bail us out of our circumstances, but He comes looking for the fruit of the earth. He has paid a heavy price. The seed for this vine was His Son, Jesus Christ. This is why, when speaking of His impending death, Jesus Christ said, *"Unless a grain of wheat falls into the ground and dies it remains alone. But if it dies it produces much fruit."* We need to be the mature bride created as His helper to accomplish His purpose in the earth and in us. Our aspiration should be His aspiration. Our desire should be to make ourselves pleasing to Him. This alone will hasten His return and provide us with a blessing when He comes.

> *Let us be glad and rejoice and give Him glory, for the marriage of the Lamb has come, and His wife has made herself ready." And to her it was granted to be arrayed in fine linen, clean and bright, for the fine linen is the righteous acts of the saints.* (Revelation 19:7-8)

We need to be mindful of the fact that God, as the husbandman, makes periodic inspections of His vineyard. Visitations are not just times of refreshing but times of judgment. When He doesn't like what He sees, He sends forth His judgment to purge and purify for the next phase of development. God judges the earth and also His house. The most evident example was in the time of Christ. He came to His own, and they did not receive Him. The words spoken by Jesus Christ became a witness against them. In Matthew 24, Jesus Christ announced His impending judgment consummated by the destruction of Jerusalem and the scattering of the people by the Romans in 70 AD. How sad that the ones who have an expectation of what God will do often miss what He is actually doing. The judgment on Jerusalem was the result of not knowing the day of their visitation!

As Christians, we must understand how God looks at the earth. We are the apple or "pupil" of His eyes. This means God sees the world through the lens of the church. We tend to look at what is going on in the world from our perspective rather than God's. This is why we want to point the finger of judgment at the world. Then we focus on how bad the world is as the sign of the end of the age. God tells us first we should judge ourselves. The world will be judged, but so will we. Our judgment is onto life; their judgment is onto condemnation. If we judge ourselves and separate ourselves from the world, we will not be a part of their judgment. This is the practical purpose of the Lord's Supper. As we regularly examine ourselves, we can escape the judgment upon the nations through self-examination and self-judgment.

> But let a man examine himself, and so let him eat of the bread and drink of the cup. For he who eats and drinks in an unworthy manner eats and drinks judgment to himself, not discerning the Lord's body. For this reason many are weak and sick among you, and many sleep. For if we would judge ourselves, we would not be judged. But when we are judged, we are chastened by the Lord, that we may not be condemned with the world. (1 Corinthians 11:28-32)

Notice, we may escape judgment, but we must understand the judgment of God is a necessary side of the eternal purpose of God. The difference between us and the world is *their* judgment is for condemnation, to damn or place a sentence upon; *ours* is for purification and purging, to achieve a better end result.

This is what Jesus Christ was referring to when He spoke of the Father pruning His vine. If a branch is unfruitful, He will cut it off. Even when it is fruitful, He will prune it to produce more fruit and to bring forth better fruit. This process of pruning is a vital part of the purpose of divine visitations. This is why when the Lord is moving, you will see growth and loss at the same time. The growth is the result of the new work of God. The loss is the result of the pruning shears of God. God's way seems sloppy to us. When we

163

think of pruning, we think of a husbandman going into the vineyard with just the right tools meticulously and carefully removing the parts that need to be pruned. Remember, the natural world is our example since the same creator is at work. God doesn't prune with human tools. God prunes with the wind. Ever notice after a storm how all the weak trees and branches are removed? This is God's way of pruning.

Another example in nature that shows this principle in action is a forest fire. When I was a kid growing up, they would put public service announcements on television to remind us to be very careful when outdoors so we didn't cause forest fires. Smokey the Bear, an animated bear, was the spokesman for the cause. There was also a well known movie by Walt Disney called *Bambi* that told the story of a small deer whose parents were killed in a forest fire to engrave the concern in young minds. Over many years, forest ecologists realized there was a big problem with this plan. Forest fires, although very destructive, are indeed a part of the natural order. People are not the only culprits in forest fires; nature causes its share as well. Forest fires provide part of the cycle of purging in the natural world, and the lack of a fire hinders the natural order. Some trees can only reproduce with intense heat, and some plants grow out of control without the occasional fire. The worse news is that without the occasional burning of the underbrush, when fires do occur they are so intense they ultimately do worse damage and are destructive without being beneficial.

This exemplifies the spiritual principles of God! We are always trying to manage our world to limit problems, and we are just causing more problems. In our management of things, we often make things much worse. Remember, the eternal God is always building for the long term result. In our immaturity, we have always felt it necessary to create perfect and protected environments. We have tried to create church environments where no one gets offended, and when offences come we agree with people when they say they want God and not church. God is building the church so those outside the church, nursing their wounds, will not get encouragement in their petty complaints but will instead be admonished to move forward through the trials of experience until God's perfect work is accomplished in them. When sin is revealed in the church, instead of thinking the world is falling apart, we should know the hand of God is at work.

Remember, failure is not an insurmountable problem for God. We need to remind ourselves of this because during times of pruning and purification, failure and human weakness seem to abound. Ask the apostle Peter. Jesus said, "Satan has desired to sift you as wheat, but when you return strengthen the brethren." He wasn't saying after you return to church. He was saying after you return to your senses. We hate messes in church and are always hiding things or trying to run the sinners out of church. At times, like in the case of Peter, we can only see who we really are when we fail. The moment we discover our heart attitude and turn to the Lord, change will come. It is funny we are so surprised to find sin in church. It is the one thing I have found common in every church. We should not take an accommodating attitude towards sin, but we should understand human failure often precedes the revealing of the glory of the Lord.

> The glory of the LORD shall be revealed, And all flesh shall see it together; For the mouth of the LORD has spoken." The voice said, "Cry out!" And he said, "What shall I cry?" "All flesh is grass, And all its loveliness is like the flower of the field. The grass withers, the flower fades, Because the breath of the LORD blows upon it; Surely the people are grass. The grass withers, the flower fades, But the word of our God stands forever." (Isaiah 40:5-8)

Please note, in this process the devil actually can be the tool of God's work. As it was in the garden, the devil's work simply reveals the works of man. The purging process will make evident the flesh works God wants to remove from His people. These works will often be works we have offered to God that were not works He commissioned. Although we often find these judgment times taxing, in the end, we will find deliverance in them.

165

> *For no other foundation can anyone lay than that which is laid, which is Jesus Christ. Now if anyone builds on this foundation with gold, silver, precious stones, wood, hay, straw, each one's work will become clear; for the Day will declare it, because it will be revealed by fire; and the fire will test each one's work, of what sort it is. If anyone's work which he has built on it endures, he will receive a reward. If anyone's work is burned, he will suffer loss; but he himself will be saved, yet so as through fire.* (1 Corinthians 3:11-15)

This process has often taken place in the history of the unfolding of God's eternal plan. Sometimes the fires have burned so hot it seemed like nothing was left. When you look at things from a strictly human perspective, you will miss the progress that will only become evident as the new life begins to bud forth. Like in the natural forests, after a fire the new life can spring forth unhindered. The seeds hidden under the former brush will begin to spring forth with new life, not only unhindered, but often fertilized by the residue of ashes from the fire. Out of death will spring forth new life. I have seen this happen in the lives of individuals, and I have seen it occur in church history. Sometimes it seems like in the darkest of times, when death is everywhere, God sends the fresh rain of revival, and great things begin to happen.

When I was a kid, I loved to study history and was especially intrigued with China. I remember reading about when the communists took over the country and began to persecute the church and expel all the missionaries. How hopeless things appeared, but the seeds were planted in the ground. Twenty years later, during the Cultural Revolution, things seemed to go from bad to worse. Without us realizing it, although the church was suffering, God was also breaking down cultural and religious barriers built over thousands of years that had hindered the early missionary works. Now in recent years, we hear the sound of great things occurring in China. Some estimate the church at over 130 million people. Now, the government is beginning to see the value of a religiously trained people, and all of a sudden the world is changing. The church coming out of those years of suffering could put the pampered church of the west to shame. The fire of tribulation has made it possible for a quick move, and seeds of life are sprouting everywhere. Oh the power and wisdom of God!

From a human perspective, this process is not only messy but far too long for us. We want everything to happen immediately. We think the faster the better. This was the attitude of the followers of Jesus Christ. He tried to warn them of the dangers of trying to rush God or put Him on our timetable.

> Now as they heard these things, He spoke another parable, because He was near Jerusalem and because they thought the kingdom of God would appear immediately. Therefore He said: "A certain nobleman went into a far country to receive for himself a kingdom and to return. So he called ten of his servants, delivered to them ten minas, and said to them, 'Do business till I come.' (Luke 19:11-13)

God has called us to the business of His kingdom. In order to be successful, we must be willing to work according to the principles of His kingdom. It should start with us trying to recognize God's principles as He has worked with them from the beginning rather than interpreting history from our own carnal thinking. It is time to move to the highest level of the will of God. This can only happen if we allow our minds to be changed by the power of God rather than conforming God to our worldly mindsets.

> I beseech you therefore, brethren, by the mercies of God, that you present your bodies a living sacrifice, holy, acceptable to God, which is your reasonable service. And do not be conformed to this world, but be transformed by the renewing of your mind, that you may prove what is that good and acceptable and perfect will of God. (Romans 12:1-2)

Again, it is important to see the principle of first the natural then the spiritual. God has chosen to work through the natural process not outside of it. This is why the work is often sloppy and complicated to us. We always want God to bypass the natural process to expedite it. We want God to pour the rain of His Spirit to such an extent it overrules the natural elements. We want God to simply cause everything to happen without the human connection. God will not violate the order He has established. It is time for us to see and understand God's way so we can walk in the "super" natural power of God! In the end, this supernatural power of God will manifest itself through us allowing us to be the blessing God has called us to be to the nations of the earth.

In Ezekiel 47, we see a beautiful, prophetic picture of what God wants to do in the earth. It begins by showing the throne of God. From the throne flows a river. Wherever this river flows life will begin to grow. The final picture is the trees of life that will be drawing life from the river but in turn giving that life to the world around them.

> *Along the bank of the river, on this side and that, will grow all kinds of trees used for food; their leaves will not wither, and their fruit will not fail. They will bear fruit every month, because their water flows from the sanctuary. Their fruit will be for food, and their leaves for medicine.* (Ezekiel 47:12)

The Tree of Life is still in the plan of God. That tree, of course, is manifested in Jesus Christ to provide life for all of us. Once we partake of that life, then we can become a tree of life. The church has always been motivated by soul winning. When we become the trees of life God has purposed us to be, we will have the greatest strategy for soul winning.

> *The fruit of the righteous is a tree of life, And he who wins souls is wise.* (Proverbs 11:30)

During the Pentecostal/charismatic movements, the church rejoiced in the river of God. People went everywhere looking for the life of the river of God. Everywhere the river went there was life. The Pentecostal movement, comprising about 13 million people in the 1960s, blossomed into a contingent of about 500 million people in only forty years. Truly the river brought life to many different denominations. Now it is time for the next wave of God. This wave will be the people of God. It will be a people who have not only tasted of the life of God but are now manifesting this life to the world!

Now that we have seen God's work in producing fruit, what then is our role? Jesus Christ said:

> *Abide in Me, and I in you. As the branch cannot bear fruit of itself, unless it abides in the vine, neither can you, unless you abide in Me. "I am the vine, you are the branches. He who abides in Me, and I in him, bears much fruit; for without Me you can do nothing.* (John 15:4-5)

The fruit of the spirit is not the work of the flesh. Although, when we see what the fruit of the spirit is, we should try to walk in it; we should also understand the fruit of the spirit comes from the life of Christ not the life of man. If you want to bear the fruit of the spirit, then your first need is to see that true life comes through Jesus Christ. One of the purposes of failure, as in the process that worked in the apostle Peter, is to show us the fruit God is looking for will not come from us but from God. Peter saw the work of God proceeding from his own resources, but in the time of his failure, he became painfully aware the fruit of God will only come from the Spirit of God.

Secondly, Jesus says:

> *If you abide in Me, and My words abide in you, you will ask what you desire, and it shall be done for you. By this My Father is glorified, that you bear much fruit; so you will be My disciples.* (John 15:7-8)

If we want to bring forth the fruit of the spirit, it must come from the Spirit and the Word of God. It is the Word that abides forever. Lasting fruit requires the work of the Word of God. As we submit to the Word, the corrective Word will produce the fruit of the spirit. The fruit comes when we are trained by the chastening hand of the Father.

> *Furthermore, we have had human fathers who corrected us, and we paid them respect. Shall we not much more readily be in subjection to the Father of spirits and live? For they indeed for a few days chastened us as seemed best to them, but He for our profit, that we may be partakers of His holiness. Now no chastening seems to be joyful for the present, but painful; nevertheless, afterward it yields the peaceable fruit of righteousness to those who have been trained by it.* (Hebrews 12:9-11)

When describing the change in the apostle Peter from the failure of denying Christ to the great preacher on the day of Pentecost, many people think this was simply the power of the Holy Spirit that came upon him. This neglects the important lesson Jesus Christ gave him when He returned in forty days after the resurrection. In John 21, Jesus is speaking to Peter about his call to ministry. Jesus says three times, "Peter, if you love me feed my sheep." Peter is still confident and even cocky about his commitment to Jesus even though he had miserably failed Him. This is amply demonstrated by the fact he is still comparing himself to others. Look how he responds when Jesus tries to deal with him.

> *Then Peter, turning around, saw the disciple whom Jesus loved following, who also had leaned on His breast at the supper, and said, "Lord, who is the one who betrays You?" Peter, seeing him, said to Jesus, "But Lord, what about this man?" Jesus said to him, "If I will that he remain till I come, what is that to you? You follow Me."* (John 21:20-22)

Peter must have responded to this correction since in the book of Acts Peter and John became a team. Peter must have dealt with his heart so he could have the "peaceable" fruit of righteousness. He not only was doing the right thing but he was at peace with the brethren rather than in conflict with them.

170

Now Peter and John went up together to the temple at the hour of prayer, the ninth hour. (Acts 3:1)

When the fruit of God is fully manifested in us, our ability to get along will be the sign of our maturity. We will not be filled with strife and debate but will work together for the purpose of God.

And I, brethren, could not speak to you as to spiritual people but as to carnal, as to babes in Christ. I fed you with milk and not with solid food; for until now you were not able to receive it, and even now you are still not able; for you are still carnal. For where there are envy, strife, and divisions among you, are you not carnal and behaving like mere men? For when one says, "I am of Paul," and another, "I am of Apollos," are you not carnal? (1 Corinthians 3:1-4)

This again leads us to the love factor addressed in the last chapter.

As the Father loved Me, I also have loved you; abide in My love. If you keep My commandments, you will abide in My love, just as I have kept My Father's commandments and abide in His love. These things I have spoken to you, that My joy may remain in you, and that your joy may be full. This is My commandment, that you love one another as I have loved you. (John 15:9-12)

If you look at the attributes of love spoken of in the book of 1 Corinthians 13, you will notice they are the attributes of the fruit of the spirit. It is truly time for love to manifest through us as it did through Jesus Christ. This place of love will manifest in a new level of relationship with God, new authority in prayer, and the full manifestation of the fruit of God in our lives.

Greater love has no one than this, than to lay down one's life for his friends. You are My friends if you do whatever I

171

command you. No longer do I call you servants, for a servant does not know what his master is doing; but I have called you friends, for all things that I heard from My Father I have made known to you. You did not choose Me, but I chose you and appointed you that you should go and bear fruit, and that your fruit should remain, that whatever you ask the Father in My name He may give you. These things I command you, that you love one another. (John 15:13-17)

In Summary

Jesus told us that the best way to discern the time of God was to watch for fruit. In determining the end time, we must be looking for the same fruit that God is. There are two harvests in the earth: one that pertains to God's plan and the other that is the result of the fruit of man's labor. The Bible says that Jesus is the vine. When we are looking for fruit we need to look at the fruit of that vine. It is only when the Father has His fruit that the end will come.

We look at a visitation from God as God bringing something to us. When God comes to visit, we need to understand He comes looking for something. Our desire should be when He comes that He sees we have prepared something for Him. Visitations are not just times of refreshing but times of judgment. When He doesn't like what He sees, He sends forth His judgment to purge and purify for the next phase of development. God judges the earth and also His house.

We must understand the judgment of God is a necessary side of the eternal purpose of God. The difference between us and the world is their judgment is for condemnation, to damn or place a sentence upon; ours is for purification and purging, to achieve a better end result. God has a pruning process where He cuts away what is unfruitful. Even when it is fruitful, He will prune it to allow more fruit and to bring forth better fruit.

When sin is revealed in the church, we should know the hand of God is at work. Failure is not an insurmountable problem for God. During times of pruning and purification, failure and human weakness seem to abound. Human failure often precedes the revealing of the glory of the Lord. It seems like in the darkest of times, when death is everywhere, God sends the fresh rain of revival, and great things begin to happen.

We want God to do everything fast and with no pain. God has a natural order and He will not violate that order. Just like nature creates havoc in our world, sometimes the work of God is messy. In the end, the supernatural power of God will manifest itself through us allowing us to be the blessing God has called us to be to the nations of the earth. The key is the Tree of Life manifested in Jesus Christ that provides life to all of us. Once we partake of that life, than we can become a tree of life manifesting this life to the world.

Chapter Twelve

WHAT DOES WALKING IN GOD'S AUTHORITY REALLY MEAN?

Now behold, one came and said to Him, "Good Teacher, what good thing shall I do that I may have eternal life?" So He said to him, "Why do you call Me good? No one is good but One, that is, God. But if you want to enter into life, keep the commandments." (Matthew 19:16-17)

For many years, the church has been driven by the desire to be good. In following this desire, a person needs to define what good is. This was the mindset of the rich young ruler who came to Jesus Christ. He wanted to define good so He could figure out how to measure up. Jesus made it very clear that you can't measure your goodness because only God is good. No one should be bold or arrogant enough to compare themselves to God. When speaking of human goodness, the Scripture is very clear.

The voice said, Cry. And he said, What shall I cry? All flesh is grass, and all the goodliness thereof is as the flower of the field: The grass withereth, the flower fadeth: because the spirit of the LORD bloweth upon it: surely the people is grass. The grass withereth, the flower fadeth: but the word of our God shall stand for ever. (Isaiah 40:6-8 KJV)

It is very clear here. Any attempt at goodness on our part will only be a temporary effort. Sooner or later our attempts will fade away because goodness is not intrinsic to the human nature.

Many people will take their understanding of the Word as stated here and create a theology based upon our inability to be good without denying the need for the pursuit of being good. The idea is that we must try to be good, but in the end we will fail. This is where grace comes in. Grace makes up for our lack. The problem with this faulty theology is its basic premise: our goal is to be good. I believe this is the result of man eating from the tree of the knowledge of good and evil. Since the garden, our efforts have been influenced by this motivation. This is the problem with knowledge given before the appointed time. This also demonstrates we are still motivated to go down the path of good and evil rather than the path God has laid out for us. It is time we got off the path of good and evil and start walking the path of God. This path will be the path of Christ and will lead us to the destiny God has laid out for us. The destiny ordained by God is the destiny of becoming like Christ, fulfilling our destiny as the sons of God in the earth.

> *And He Himself gave some to be apostles, some prophets, some evangelists, and some pastors and teachers, for the equipping of the saints for the work of ministry, for the edifying of the body of Christ, till we all come to the unity of the faith and of the knowledge of the Son of God, to a perfect man, to the measure of the stature of the fullness of Christ; that we should no longer be children, tossed to and fro and carried about with every wind of doctrine, by the trickery of men, in the cunning craftiness of deceitful plotting, but, speaking the truth in love, may grow up in all things into Him who is the head — Christ — (Ephesians 4:11-15)*

This corresponds to the message that we must grow up and not be children. When children are young, it is hard to explain things to them. It is easier just to teach them good things versus bad things. Children don't always know what it means to be bad; but through our words and behavior, the concept sticks and sends them on the journey of evaluating themselves as being either good or bad. This is the story of the children of Israel in the Old Testament. God gave them the law to help them find the good life. It is clear from the Scriptures that the goal of the law was to give people prosperity and success. The law would set them apart as God's special people and would give them a life that would be a witness to the world. This attitude would have taken them into the "Promised Land" with an opportunity for long lasting success and blessing in life. This is why the Lord gave this admonition to the leader of the people, Joshua.

> *Only be strong and very courageous, that you may observe to do according to all the law which Moses My servant commanded you; do not turn from it to the right hand or to the left, that you may prosper wherever you go. This Book of the Law shall not depart from your mouth, but you shall meditate in it day and night, that you may observe to do according to all that is written in it. For then you will make your way prosperous, and then you will have good success.* (Joshua 1:7-8)

How different this is even from the modern Christian notion of the laws of God. We often see the law to be a burden the people could not bear, so God simply got rid of it. Time had proven keeping it was an impossible task.

I am not espousing the keeping of all the law of Moses. It is obvious from the Scriptures that the religious observations were picture examples of the time to come. Many of the laws of Moses were civil laws not meant to be taken into the new order based upon the kingdom of God. The kingdom fulfills the promise of God to Abraham that his seed would be a blessing in every nation of the earth. The kingdom order gives us the ability to function in many different nations and groups of people. Many of the religious ceremonies in the law taught things about cleanliness and good behavior that had far reaching implications the children of Israel could not have understood. The law is for the servants not the sons, but the principles of the law should certainly be recognized and honored. We must also see the law was not to find out who was good or bad but to teach and train the people of God for the day of maturity. In their maturity they would be able to follow the law of the Spirit rather than the letter of the law. It was meant to lead them to the greater day God yet had for His children.

> *For on the one hand there is an annulling of the former commandment because of its weakness and unprofitableness, for the law made nothing perfect; on the other hand, there is the bringing in of a better hope, through which we draw near to God.* (Hebrews 7:18-19)

This word "perfect" has nothing to do with being good. God is good. Perfection means you are growing to maturity, and with maturity comes greater responsibility. The problem with the former mindset so prevalent among Evangelical Christians is that when we promote an unattainable goal it isn't long before people give up. In contemporary society, we have decided God accepts us the way we are, so why try to be anything different? When we understand the goal is attainable, we will be more inclined to press towards it. We must also understand the acceptance of God is not the end game but the beginning of our journey. Once confident in God's love, we can go forward and know our failures are not about losing out on God but are an obstacle God will help us overcome.

We will also be motivated by the desire for maturity knowing it is not only the Father's purpose but maturity helps us obtain the best life we possibly can. I included the chapter in this book on how God works through and includes the natural as a part of His plan because we need to see how important it is to manifest our spiritual life in the natural world. I have observed that people are strongly motivated by a need for purpose. Purpose is a God given drive. If we lower the bar for people, the natural drive for purpose becomes circumvented. Keeping the bar higher causes us to increase our expectation and encourages us to press forward. This is what motivated the apostle Paul to face difficulty knowing that a better life awaited him

Not that I have already attained, or am already perfected; but I press on, that I may lay hold of that for which Christ Jesus has also laid hold of me. Brethren, I do not count myself to have apprehended; but one thing I do, forgetting those things which are behind and reaching forward to those things which are ahead, I press toward the goal for the prize of the upward call of God in Christ Jesus. (Philippians 3:12-14)

It is important to note that Jesus Christ did not separate the need for keeping His commandments from our Christian walk. Jesus said, *"If you want to enter into life, keep the commandments."* When looking at the apostle Paul's motivation, it was twofold. Eternal life was set before him, but he also included the need for perfection in fulfilling his destiny on the earth. We have learned God has put eternity in our heart, and with this we also see the corresponding motivation for purpose. We need to bring these two motivations together, understanding how we have been given God ordained motivations to fulfill His purpose. The desire for purpose will fulfill our earthly call. The desire for eternity will motivate us to our heavenly call. We need to have both motivations. When speaking to the rich, young ruler in the account recorded in the gospel of Mark, Jesus Christ pointed him to eternal things but did not discount the earthly manifestation of God's blessing.

So Jesus answered and said, "Assuredly, I say to you, there is no one who has left house or brothers or sisters or father or mother or wife or children or lands, for My sake and the gospel's, who shall not receive a hundredfold now in this time — houses and brothers and sisters and mothers and children and lands, with persecutions — and in the age to come, eternal life. (Mark 10:29-30)

Many people live only for the present life. This life is usually filled with self centered motivations, living only in the flesh. Unfortunately, many Christians motivated by the call of eternity fail to grasp the accompanying need for purpose. These Christians will also be carnal and flesh motivated or will simply have a religious life disconnected from everyday life. Because of the lack of understanding on how to live in this world, many powerful movements of God stagnated into carnally motivated institutions. No one knew what to do after the fervor of the initial move dissipated. Recent moves were highly motivated by the expectation of the return of Christ. Since He obviously hasn't returned, the fervor of expectation was lost. This fervor is often substituted for formal religion, fleshly behavior, or carnal understanding.

If we are to fulfill the Father's purpose, we must be fully committed to two calls: the eternal and the temporal. God's intentions, although eternal in the end, certainly speak of a dramatic impact on the world. Jesus Christ was God becoming flesh and dwelling among us. God wants us to bring Him into our lives. He wants us to "dwell" in the world so His witness can be seen and not just heard. This is the only way we will fulfill our purpose and God's desire to cause all nations of the world to witness the glory of God in His people. It will be the finale of God's presentation to the world.

> *Now it shall come to pass in the latter days That the mountain of the LORD's house Shall be established on the top of the mountains, And shall be exalted above the hills; And all nations shall flow to it.* (Isaiah 2:2)

Not only will we be a light but the prophet Isaiah declares kings will come to the brightness of our rising.

> *The Gentiles shall come to your light, And kings to the brightness of your rising.* (Isaiah 60:3)

Usually when God begins to move in a special way, it is the poor and disenfranchised who initially come. The rest come only when they see the witness and the success of the venture. This might sound strange to speak of the kingdom from this perspective, but it is very true. God begins his ventures by choosing the ones no one else would choose. The disciples understood this for they understood even among themselves that God had not chosen the learned and skilled but the ones with a heart after Him.

> For you see your calling, brethren, that not many wise according to the flesh, not many mighty, not many noble, are called. But God has chosen the foolish things of the world to put to shame the wise, and God has chosen the weak things of the world to put to shame the things which are mighty; (1 Corinthians 1:26-27)

Now does this principle mean God intends to keep us down so all the glory goes to Him? King David provided the testimony of God's plan. When God needed a king to replace Saul, He sent the prophet Samuel to the house of Jesse to appoint the new king. When surveying the group of Jesse's sons from a natural perspective, the choice was obvious. Eliab was an immediately recognized candidate for being the new king. God gave Samuel a warning and set him on the proper course.

> But the LORD said to Samuel, "Do not look at his appearance or at his physical stature, because I have refused him. For the LORD does not see as man sees; for man looks at the outward appearance, but the LORD looks at the heart." (1 Samuel 16:7)

God had His anointed chosen and set apart for the purpose God had called him to. He picked the lowly one whose heart was after him. Once God had made His choice, He took David to his place as king. It was not an easy ride because of God's timing, the need for Saul's sin to have its full run, and the time David needed to be ready for his purpose. The day came when David sat upon the throne and the honor and glory he gave to God was also given to him. In his latter days, David forgot where the glory originated and actually thought He could do something for God from his resources and success. God's response was obvious and direct.

> *Now therefore, thus shall you say to My servant David, 'Thus says the LORD of hosts: "I took you from the sheepfold, from following the sheep, to be ruler over My people Israel. And I have been with you wherever you have gone, and have cut off all your enemies from before you, and have made you a name like the name of the great men who are on the earth.* (1 Chronicles 17:7-8)

David wanted to build God a house; and the response of God was, *"Have I ever spoken a word to anyone from the tribes of Israel, whom I commanded to shepherd my people, saying why have you not built me a house of cedar?"* In other words, we should not try to do something for God He has not asked for. We should never think we are the source God draws from. God draws from His own resources. Although David was not allowed to take God's initiative, his obedience and commitment to God had brought him great honor and glory in the natural. This is a pattern God wants for all His people. Did you know God has called us all to be priests and kings?

> *And they sang a new song, saying: "You are worthy to take the scroll, And to open its seals; For You were slain, And have redeemed us to God by Your blood Out of every tribe and tongue and people and nation, And have made us kings and priests to our God; And we shall reign on the earth."* (Revelation 5:9-10)

A priest is one who ministers between God and the people. As Christians, we should see ourselves as God's emissaries to the world. We are all priests and should take this responsibility seriously according to how God wants to use us to be His contact with other people. As kings, we have a different focus. This has to do with our ability to exercise authority in the world. God has chosen us for a place of authority and dominion from the beginning. Just as it was with King David, the heart is the foundation of our call and must never be forgotten. But we must also see how God has set us on the journey to walk in authority in this life. We must understand how to walk the path to our authority. This is where our earthly purpose and motivation becomes essential.

When speaking about manifesting the light of God to our world, we need to understand what that is. When I was a kid, we sang a song that said, "This little light of mine, I'm going to let it shine." We would hold a finger in the air like a candle and move it around like we were trying to take our light somewhere. Jesus came as the light of the world and told His disciples that we are called to be the children of the light. Jesus said we need to shine our light and not hide it because the world needs the influence and witness of the sons of God. How do we manifest the light? We manifest the light by our behavior.

> *Let your light so shine before men, that they may see your good works and glorify your Father in heaven.* (Matthew 5:16)

We have a responsibility to our world. We must show them the light of God's Word demonstrated in our lives so they can see the power of the Word in action. Jesus Christ was the Word made flesh. That is also the call God has for us.

Even though our desire to please God requires proper conduct, we should understand how to relate to that call from the New Testament order. In the old covenant the rituals they followed made the people sin conscious. Consciousness of the law will not bring us to perfection. This is clear from the Scriptures.

> *Therefore, if perfection were through the Levitical priesthood (for under it the people received the law), what further need was there that another priest should rise according to the order of Melchizedek, and not be called according to the order of Aaron?* (Hebrews 7:11)

When Jesus Christ came and offered the final sacrifice for sin, He wanted to remove the consciousness of sin from us so we could pursue God without fear, shame, or a sense of lack. In the old covenant, the continual offering of the sacrifices also constantly reminded the people of their sin. Sin consciousness will hold us back from going to the place God has for us. When we accept the sacrifice of God, we become God conscious rather than self conscious and are able to go on to the place of perfection God has for us.

> *Therefore, brethren, having boldness to enter the Holiest by the blood of Jesus, by a new and living way which He consecrated for us, through the veil, that is, His flesh, and having a High Priest over the house of God, let us draw near with a true heart in full assurance of faith, having our hearts sprinkled from an evil conscience and our bodies washed with pure water.* (Hebrews 10:19-22)

The goal of taking away our sin consciousness was not so we could sin without guilt. It was so we could live for Christ without guilt. In the natural family, the good boy/ bad boy instruction many children are taught leaves them with a lifetime of shame and guilt. God doesn't want to do that with His children. He wants us to learn right and wrong so we can live life with the ability to make positive decisions. He wants us to have the abundant life.

> *I am the door. If anyone enters by Me, he will be saved, and will go in and out and find pasture. The thief does not come except to steal, and to kill, and to destroy. I have come that they may have life, and that they may have it more abundantly.* (John 10:9-10)

When I take the place of being the "king" in the nations of God, I will need to think like one. A king doesn't set his goal to be good but to be wise and make the right choices. A king needs to order his life with his position in mind. Lemuel was a king who received council from His mother about the responsibility of his position.

> *It is not for kings, O Lemuel, It is not for kings to drink wine, Nor for princes intoxicating drink; Lest they drink and forget the law, And pervert the justice of all the afflicted. Give strong*

drink to him who is perishing, And wine to those who are bitter of heart. Let him drink and forget his poverty, And remember his misery no more. (Proverbs 31:4-7)

This advice gives an opportunity for an interesting mindset change. Since He would need to make the right decisions and live according to the law, she urges him to stay away from alcoholic beverages. Why? Alcohol is a drug that diminishes our ability to think. Wine and strong drink would have an influence, taking away his full capacity to make a choice. In evangelical churches there is a lot of discussion about the use of alcohol. The discussion is always made from the viewpoint of whether drinking alcohol is a sin or not. If I am mature and recognize my role of responsibility, I must see why God has brought me past sin consciousness. Many of our choices in life are not sin issues but choices for wisdom and discretion. Look what the Scriptures tell us about liquor and wine.

Wine is a mocker, Strong drink is a brawler, And whoever is led astray by it is not wise. The wrath of a king is like the roaring of a lion; Whoever provokes him to anger sins against his own life. (Proverbs 20:1-2)

The Scripture says the use of alcohol or any drug that can influence our behavior is not wise. In other words, drinking makes you stupid. Even an intelligent and normally controlled person, can be influenced by this drug. One thing it often does is provoke emotional behavior, like anger; and the king who partakes of alcohol could use their authority in the wrong way. The king could kill somebody and get away with it. King David proved this point; but we also see how, in the end of his life, he could not fulfill his heart's desire to build God a house because he had become a man of war. Too many Christians have the immature attitude that if it isn't "unlawful" it is okay. Like King David, many sincere Christians who have a heart for God are missing out on the things God has for them because they do not think with responsibility. Many people are like children, if their parents haven't said anything or if nobody is watching, they will do what they want not what is best or the responsible thing to do. We need to be mindful of more than our immediate desire. Leadership demands we think about the long term implications of our choices. This is what the admonition concerning alcohol tells us.

> *Who has woe? Who has sorrow? Who has contentions? Who has complaints? Who has wounds without cause? Who has redness of eyes? Those who linger long at the wine, Those who go in search of mixed wine. Do not look on the wine when it is red, When it sparkles in the cup, When it swirls around smoothly; At the last it bites like a serpent, And stings like a viper. Your eyes will see strange things, And your heart will utter perverse things.* (Proverbs 23:29-33)

Keep in mind; this is not just a discussion on drinking. It is an embodiment of thinking that would replace being a "sin conscious" people with being a people of maturity and authority who want to exercise their rights by thinking about others not themselves. We need to be people who think about the long term implications of our choices not just people thinking about our immediate desire. As kings in the earth, we must turn from the simple and begin to seek out the deep things of God, turning to Him with our whole hearts. God is looking for honorable kings who will take their place and live a life that will bring glory to God and to them. It is no coincidence that God spent so much time telling us about the kings He placed over His people. As with all Scripture, it is given for our example for we are all called to be a nation of kings for our God in the earth!

> *It is the glory of God to conceal a matter, But the glory of kings is to search out a matter. As the heavens for height and the earth for depth, So the heart of kings is unsearchable. Take away the dross from silver, And it will go to the silversmith for jewelry. Take away the wicked from before the king, And his throne will be established in righteousness.* (Proverbs 25:2-5)

In Summary

Many Christians who are trying to follow God are trying to be good. God does not want us to focus on being good. God wants us to focus on becoming His mature sons in the earth. We must see that the law was not to find out who was good or bad but to teach and train the people of God for the day of maturity. In their maturity they would be able to follow the law of the Spirit rather than the letter of the law. Perfection means you are growing to maturity, and with maturity comes greater responsibility.

When we promote an unattainable goal, it isn't long before people give up. When we understand the goal is attainable, we will be more inclined to press towards it. In contemporary society, we have decided God accepts us the way we are, so why try to be anything different? It is important to note that Jesus Christ did not separate the need for keeping His commandments from our Christian walk. Jesus said, "If you want to enter into life, keep the commandments."

We must not forget that God is a God of purpose. We must understand that to fulfill our purpose we must be committed to two calls: the eternal and the temporal. When we obey the laws of God, there is a blessing in the temporal that impacts the world. The world sees that there is a difference between those who follow God and those who do not. This is the only way we will fulfill our purpose and God's desire to cause all nations of the world to witness the glory of God in His people.

God has called us to be priests and kings. A priest is one who ministers between God and the people. We are all priests and should take this responsibility seriously according to how God wants to use us to be His contact with other people. As kings, we have a different focus. This has to do with our ability to exercise authority in the world. We must understand how to walk the path to our authority. To walk in authority, we must be God conscious not sin conscious. The goal of taking away our sin consciousness is not so we can sin without guilt. It was so we could live for Christ without guilt. Since we are called to be a king, we must understand that a king doesn't set his goal to be good but to be wise and make the right choices. A king needs to order his life with his position in mind. Many of our choices in life are not sin issues but choices for wisdom and discretion. Leadership demands we think about the long term implications of our choices. God is looking for honorable kings who will take their place and live a life that will bring glory to God and to them.

Chapter Thirteen

How Do You Activate Wisdom?

Those who are wise shall shine Like the brightness of the firmament, And those who turn many to righteousness Like the stars forever and ever. (Daniel 12:3)

There was a time in the history of the children of Israel when they came under the judgment of God. The tool of God's judgment was the city-state of Babylon. Because they did not obey the voice of God and walk in the ways He had for them, God sent Babylon into their country to destroy the Holy City and the temple. God had forewarned them through the prophet Moses that if they rebelled against God and failed to keep His covenant, He would punish them by allowing the neighboring countries to overpower them. He also spoke of their disbursement throughout the nations of the world. When Babylon came into the land of Israel, they took back to Babylon the treasuries of the house of God and what they considered the cream of the crop among the people. Included in this group were Daniel and several companions. These were consecrated followers of God who maintained their relationship with God and His covenant during the time of their captivity. This became a witness to Babylon and their king, Nebuchadnezzar. It would be in the midst of this bondage that God would reveal His power and authority through His people. It is an important lesson to understand about the power of God. We do not need to be in control of our surroundings to manifest the authority God has for us. It is in the midst of these times that we need to see God has called us to rule in the middle of our trouble.

> *The LORD shall send the rod of Your strength out of Zion. Rule in the midst of Your enemies! Your people shall be volunteers In the day of Your power; In the beauties of holiness, from the womb of the morning, You have the dew of Your youth. The LORD has sworn And will not relent, "You are a priest forever According to the order of Melchizedek." (Psalm 110:2-4)*

Melchizedek was not just the priest of the Lord. His name means, "king of Salem or king of peace." He did not have an earthly kingdom but walked in the authority of heaven. This is why the book of Daniel is such a beautiful picture of the plan of God. It shows us that God's servants had authority and power outside the human system. Although their authority was outside the system, it operated in the midst of that system both by giving a witness of the power of God and by impacting the human system. This is the reality of what God wants to demonstrate in the world today. He wants His kingdom operating outside the human system yet with a powerful witness and a powerful influence.

This is what Jesus was speaking to His disciples about when He spoke of them being both the salt of the earth and the light of the world. Light represents something that is seen in the midst of the darkness, and salt represents having an influence or impact. God does not want us to take over the world but to be a light that will give the world something to respond to. This is why in the midst of great darkness God is calling us to arise. I believe we are living in the day when God will become more tangible. The Word is clear. God will do something to shine His light through us, and we, the church, need to recognize this as an appointed time to arise and shine and let the glory of the Lord be seen upon us.

> *Arise, shine; For your light has come! And the glory of the LORD is risen upon you. For behold, the darkness shall cover the earth, And deep darkness the people; But the LORD will arise over you, And His glory will be seen upon you. The Gen-*

tiles shall come to your light, And kings to the brightness of your rising. (Isaiah 60:1-3)

People will come to our light. It is obvious that from the beginning God has allowed a contrasting world to His kingdom. In the simplest form, the tree of knowledge of good and evil represented an alternative to God's choice. It offered the world as an alternative to the choice God had for them. What the world has to offer is not usually bad within itself. That is why the term "good and evil" applied to the tree of knowledge and applies to the world we live in today. With God, it isn't so much what is offered but how it appeals to our motivations and how it contrasts with the way God wants us to live. This is why the allure of the world is so deceptive. It is a way that appears good, but in the end it will bring death.

There is a way that seems right to a man, But its end is the way of death. Even in laughter the heart may sorrow, And the end of mirth may be grief. (Proverbs 14:12)

Man's way does not appear deadly at first. It is the end result that is deadly. These Scriptures also point out the way of man may bring laughter and mirth, but underneath there is a death and despair growing. Since God alone knows the future, we need to understand why His way is better than ours and willingly give ourselves to Him. God's concern and purpose is about the end of the matter, and we must share His purpose. Christianity is about what happens on payday not what happens during the week. If you have a job, getting up on a Monday morning may not be pleasant; but when payday comes you'll be glad you did. The person who chooses the temporary pleasure will find payday a very disappointing day.

For the wages of sin is death, but the gift of God is eternal life in Christ Jesus our Lord. (Romans 6:23)

When Daniel and his companions were carried off to Babylon, it must have been an emotionally heart wrenching time. They were the elite of Jerusalem, and now they would be carried away to a foreign land. They lost their old life. As they watched the Holy City and temple burn to the ground, it must have also been a difficult time spiritually. Upon entering the city of Babylon and seeing the impressive temples of the gods of Babylon, they would have been challenged to still believe in the power and awesomeness of their God. The true prophet Jeremiah had foretold of this judgment according to the warnings of the words given by Moses. Yet, there were many false prophets who said God would never allow judgment upon the Holy City. A good God would not allow bad things to happen to His people and certainly not to His temple. The human mind could not fathom the plan of God. This is why we need to be so careful in this day. It is going to be in the day of trouble we will need to arise. If we are not careful, we will listen to the voices based on human wisdom and reasoning and miss the voice of God.

When they arrived in Babylon, Daniel and his companions were offered an amazing proposition. If they would submit to the instruction of their new masters and eat from their table, they could have their former status back. They would once again be the elite. Now, they would be the elite of Babylon instead of the elite of God. Babylon offered immediate access to power, prestige, and affluence. What did choosing God have to offer them now? For Daniel there seemed to be no confusion. Daniel knew what He would do. Daniel was to be a man of great influence. He remained faithful to God, and God was faithful to him. God gave him favor with the person in charge of him.

> *But Daniel purposed in his heart that he would not defile himself with the portion of the king's delicacies, nor with the wine which he drank; therefore he requested of the chief of the eunuchs that he might not defile himself. Now God had brought Daniel into the favor and goodwill of the chief of the eunuchs.* (Daniel 1:8-9)

Daniel did not use God's favor for his advantage, but he used God's favor as an opportunity to shine for God. This would be the beginning of his path to great influence and his path to great wisdom and understanding.

> *The fear of the LORD is the beginning of wisdom; A good understanding have all those who do His commandments. His praise endures forever.* (Psalm 111:10)

Although the fear of the Lord appears to be something that appeals to the base part of our human nature, it actually has a foundation in logic. Fear is a deep part of our emotional response to life. In the animal kingdom, most of the natural order is built upon the fear, flight, or fight motivation. When motivated by fear in the animal realm, the creatures will either run or fight. They are not endowed with the same ability to use logic or reason as man. What separates us from the animal kingdom is not a larger brain as the evolutionist would teach. The deeper realms of understanding come from our human spirit, which is the result of the breath of life God has given to us.

> *But there is a spirit in man, And the breath of the Almighty gives him understanding. Great men are not always wise, Nor do the aged always understand justice.* (Job 32:8-9)

Although the human spirit gives us the capacity for great wisdom and understanding, it is obviously true we do not always operate in that realm. Why do we fail to operate in the level of understanding and wisdom God has gifted us in? Because when we fail to see who we are in God, we operate in the realm of the earth and often live only as animals with bigger brains. This is the danger of the theory of evolution. When we see the creation as having power within itself outside of God, we fall under the curse of living in the natural order of the creation rather than the superior order of God. Evolution makes us worshippers of the creation rather than the Creator, and it brings us under a curse.

> *because, although they knew God, they did not glorify Him as God, nor were thankful, but became futile in their thoughts,*

and their foolish hearts were darkened. Professing to be wise, they became fools, and changed the glory of the incorruptible God into an image made like corruptible man — and birds and four-footed animals and creeping things. Therefore God also gave them up to uncleanness, in the lusts of their hearts, to dishonor their bodies among themselves, who exchanged the truth of God for the lie, and worshiped and served the creature rather than the Creator, who is blessed forever. Amen. (Romans 1:21-25)

The word "fool" here speaks of becoming a simpleton or stupid. It does not mean they have a lack of intelligence or knowledge. It means their emotions or desires make intelligent decisions impossible. Daniel and his companions knew where true wisdom and understanding would come from. This wisdom would separate them from Babylon and even bring them under severe opposition, but in the end they would shine with God's wisdom. The choice that put them in hot water was also the path that would lead them to demonstrate the glory of God. The opposite path is the path of pride. Pride says, I don't need God, I don't need God's Word; and I can do what I want, when I want, and the way I want. "I" becomes god, rather than following the living God. This path will always lead to judgment.

For you have said in your heart: 'I will ascend into heaven, I will exalt my throne above the stars of God; I will also sit on the mount of the congregation On the farthest sides of the north; I will ascend above the heights of the clouds, I will be like the Most High.' Yet you shall be brought down to Sheol, To the lowest depths of the Pit. (Isaiah 14:13-15)

To live outside the life of God, is to live outside true understanding. No matter how intelligent a thought seems, it becomes tainted when it is outside the mind and will of God. Once outside the mind and will of God, our choices become stupefied by our desires, feelings, and natural motivations. We are called to live above that realm.

> *This I say, therefore, and testify in the Lord, that you should no longer walk as the rest of the Gentiles walk, in the futility of their mind, having their understanding darkened, being alienated from the life of God, because of the ignorance that is in them, because of the blindness of their heart; who, being past feeling, have given themselves over to lewdness, to work all uncleanness with greediness.* (Ephesians 4:17-19)

Outside the life of God, our hearts are hardened. The word "blindness" in the original version, speaks of a process of hardening through applying mortar. Our divine ability for understanding becomes impossible from the mortar of our deep seated human motivations. This leads to more greediness or self centeredness and unclean behavior. The word unclean is the opposite of purity. Purity of behavior will come from God.

Having a pure heart will bring us into the presence of God and bring us to the place of true wisdom and understanding. The commandments of God produce a pure heart. Without the purity of heart that comes through keeping God's commandments, even the teachers of the Word are blind.

> *Now the purpose of the commandment is love from a pure heart , from a good conscience, and from sincere faith, from which some, having strayed, have turned aside to idle talk, desiring to be teachers of the law, understanding neither what they say nor the things which they affirm.* (1 Timothy 1:5-7)

For Daniel and his companions, the persecution they were under was able to enhance their wisdom and understanding. Times of trouble are opportunities to purify ourselves before the Lord. God uses tribulation to purify His people.

And those of the people who understand shall instruct many;
yet for many days they shall fall by sword and flame, by cap-
tivity and plundering. Now when they fall, they shall be aided
with a little help; but many shall join with them by intrigue.
And some of those of understanding shall fall, to refine them,
purify them, and make them white, until the time of the end;
because it is still for the appointed time. (Daniel 11:33-35)

In the midst of this persecution, they continued to walk in obedience to the purpose God had for them. This process of purification would constantly bring up the issues of the heart. True understanding is not just a God issue but a heart issue.

O you simple ones, understand prudence, And you fools, be
of an understanding heart. (Proverbs 8:5)

If we want true understanding, we need to find our source in the Tree of Life, the only true path to understanding. We must give God our hearts. Without giving our hearts to God, all our thoughts will be stupefied. To have this understanding, we must not only give our heart to it but we must keep our hearts fixed on seeing God's wisdom and understanding as our goal.

So that you incline your ear to wisdom, And apply your heart
to understanding; Yes, if you cry out for discernment, And lift
up your voice for understanding, If you seek her as silver, And
search for her as for hidden treasures; Then you will under-
stand the fear of the LORD, And find the knowledge of God.
For the LORD gives wisdom; From His mouth come knowl-
edge and understanding; (Proverbs 2:2-6)

When Daniel and his companions set their hearts on God's wisdom, they not only benefited from this understanding but it became obvious to the people around them.

Then the king interviewed them, and among them all none
was found like Daniel, Hananiah, Mishael, and Azariah;

therefore they served before the king. And in all matters of
wisdom and understanding about which the king examined
them, he found them ten times better than all the magicians
and astrologers who were in all his realm. (Daniel 1:19-20)

When we truly walk in the wisdom and understanding of
God, people will seek us out. People came from all over the world
to witness Solomon's wisdom and to see it in operation in his kingdom. The world wants to portray the people of God as simpletons
when we are the ones who have the true source of all inspiration.
Just think, through the Spirit of God, we have access to the mind
and heart of God. We have access to the mind that created all things.
Just think about what creativity could come from the house of God,
if we would lend ourselves to Godly understanding. Our lack of
spiritual perception limits our ability to see the wisdom and the
power of God's creative thoughts.

But we speak the wisdom of God in a mystery, the hidden
wisdom which God ordained before the ages for our glory,
which none of the rulers of this age knew; for had they known,
they would not have crucified the Lord of glory. But as it is
written: "Eye has not seen, nor ear heard, Nor have entered
into the heart of man The things which God has prepared for
those who love Him." But God has revealed them to us
through His Spirit. For the Spirit searches all things, yes, the
deep things of God. (1 Corinthians 2:7-10)

These Scriptures sound like a warning to the world only. Yet
the rulers of the world, who did not see or understand what God
was doing through Christ, included the religious leaders of the time
who also consented to His crucifixion. They too were motivated by
self-centered interests and so became just as stupid as the world system. Isn't that a sad thought? They waited thousands of years for
the Messiah, and when He came they crucified Him because He
didn't fit into their program. The Word became flesh and dwelt
among them, but they didn't know who He was even though they

were devoting their lives to the teaching of the Word. This is why we need to have a "heart of understanding."

When Daniel and his companions gave themselves to God, He gave them wisdom in all their knowledge. When examined, they were found ten times better than all the astrologers and magicians. Archeological studies reveal early civilizations had an amazing knowledge of heavenly bodies. Many of the early pyramids and stone structures of early history were built around these studies, and much of the architecture amazes people today. Some have even speculated about alien visits. How about we recognize the fact that knowledge can be supernaturally inspired when the living God is involved? The highest achievements of men have always had a religious component, but we have failed in our modern times to realize the power of the spirit of man to gain understanding. We especially fail to see how the true and living God has made available to us an understanding that allows us to solve all the problems of man. Our spiritual perception should translate to knowledge in all areas of life. When will the people of God recognize this and ascend to the lofty place, instead of simply offering religiously restrained knowledge?

Astrology and magic are mocked today, but history proves they are the foundations of modern science. Daniel was a man with an understanding of dreams and visions. Although modern science disclaims the notion, let's remember their roots and see the incredible power of spiritual insight. We must be careful not to allow the thinking and practice of science to limit our belief in the supernatural power of God. Although science claims to operate solely in the rational and logical realm, many of its theories leave a great deal to faith. Science is always changing based upon the newest information and should never be seen as an exact process. It should be noted Daniel and his companions excelled among the scientific people of the time. Christians today should feel just as strongly the need to face the challenge of science. We should not do so in opposition to science but as participants who are fully willing and able to present our case. Although the world in their wisdom will look down on Christians and speak to us in a condescending way, we must always

198

understand the wisdom of the world is not God's wisdom. As in the time of Daniel, we must see God's wisdom as the superior wisdom and become God's agents to demonstrate this to the world in which we live.

For it is written: "I will destroy the wisdom of the wise, And bring to nothing the understanding of the prudent." Where is the wise? Where is the scribe? Where is the disputer of this age? Has not God made foolish the wisdom of this world? (1 Corinthians 1:19-20)

Daniel and his companions excelled in government and the highest realms of authority, and we should be so inclined today. Every field of life needs a Christian witness, and we must boldly go where no one else has gone before. When it comes to wisdom, knowledge, and understanding we should excel. Daniel and his companions did not reject the knowledge of the time; they simply put it in the perspective of God's Word. We must be careful as Christians not to shun the knowledge of our time. We have often done this, and the world got the idea we were unlearned and uneducated. If we are to confront the systems of the world, we need to meet people where they are. We should be avid in our pursuit of knowledge but with the balance of being aware of the times. God does not want us to be ignorant. He does want us to be perceptive.

of the sons of Issachar who had understanding of the times, to know what Israel ought to do, their chiefs were two hundred; and all their brethren were at their command; (1 Chronicles 12:32)

Since Daniel and his companions were taken into captivity, it is easy for us to see why they were the servants of Babylon. Yet, although we are not servants of the world, we should have the attitude we are here to serve. Daniel didn't have a slave mentality. He kept his integrity even in the face of death. But Daniel was a servant. Daniel served where God placed him, and this must be the attitude of all the sons of God. Jesus Christ gave us the example, and it should be the example we follow as our witness to the world.

> *And He said to them, "The kings of the Gentiles exercise lord-ship over them, and those who exercise authority over them are called 'benefactors.' But not so among you; on the contrary, he who is greatest among you, let him be as the younger, and he who governs as he who serves. For who is greater, he who sits at the table, or he who serves? Is it not he who sits at the table? Yet I am among you as the One who serves.* (Luke 22:25-27)

It is this attitude that will bring us to the place of preeminence God has for us. God's wisdom will manifest itself through humility and meekness. God's wisdom does not seek for self but for others. It is through this wisdom we will shine forth in the world just as Daniel and his companions in Babylon.

> *Who is wise and understanding among you? Let him show by good conduct that his works are done in the meekness of wisdom. But if you have bitter envy and self-seeking in your hearts, do not boast and lie against the truth. This wisdom does not descend from above, but is earthly, sensual, demonic. For where envy and self-seeking exist, confusion and every evil thing are there. But the wisdom that is from above is first pure, then peaceable, gentle, willing to yield, full of mercy and good fruits, without partiality and without hypocrisy. Now the fruit of righteousness is sown in peace by those who make peace.* (James 3:13-18)

In Summary

God wants His kingdom operating outside the human system, yet with a powerful witness and a powerful influence. Jesus spoke to His disciples of them being both the salt of the earth and the light of the world. Light represents something that is seen in the midst of the darkness, and salt represents having an influence or impact. God wants us to be a light that people can come to that is an alternative to the world system.

The human mind cannot fathom the plan of God. This is why we need to be so careful in this day. If we are not careful, we will listen to the voices based on human wisdom and reasoning and miss the voice of God. Although the fear of the Lord appears to be something that appeals to the base part of our human nature, it actually has a foundation in logic. Fear is a deep part of our emotional response to life. The deeper realms of understanding come from our human spirit, which is the result of the breath of life God has given to us.

Although the human spirit gives us the capacity for great wisdom and understanding, it is obviously true we do not always operate in that realm. Why do we fail to operate in the level of understanding and wisdom God has gifted us in? Because when we fail to see who we are in God, we operate in the realm of the earth and often live only as animals with bigger brains. This is the danger of the theory of evolution. When we see the creation as having power within itself outside of God, we fall under the curse of living in the natural order of the creation rather than the superior order of God. Evolution makes us worshippers of the creation rather than the Creator, and it brings us under a curse.

Chapter Fourteen

ARE YOU WILLING TO WALK AS A SON OF GOD?

For as many as are led by the Spirit of God, these are sons of God. For you did not receive the spirit of bondage again to fear, but you received the Spirit of adoption by whom we cry out, "Abba, Father. (Romans 8:14-15)

We know that from the beginning God has had a plan for man. This plan is for us to become the sons of God in the earth. As the sons of God, we will bear the image of God and fulfill the Father's purpose in the earth. This was the purpose of Jesus Christ, and this is the purpose of the sons of God in the earth today. It seems like an "out of our reach" goal. With man it would be impossible, but we know with God all things are possible. We have learned everything is possible in God, and everything must wait for the appointed time. We must be willing to wait for the time, but we must also be careful not to miss the time because we have given up hope in God's plan. As a lifelong God seeker, I never want to give up on my pursuit of God; and because of my love for Him I do not want to forsake the purpose He has for me. It is obvious God's plan for us individually will also connect us to the grand plan He has for His church.

One of the most important reasons we get off base in our pursuit of the things of God is that we quickly turn from being God centered to being man centered in our thoughts. When man chose the tree of knowledge of good and evil over the plan of God, he created a "man" centered course rather than a "God" centered one. We must be "Theocentric" and not "anthrocentric." It should be noted that the immediate response to eating from the tree of knowledge of good and evil was that they became aware of their nakedness. Self-consciousness is a sign we are partaking of the wrong tree. We can only find life by partaking of the Tree of Life. When our course is leading to Christ, it will bring the true life of God. When our course involves the pursuit of a self-centered motivation, it will bring death no matter how sincere the motives may appear. Jesus Christ has made clear to us the path of life.

> *Then He said to them all, "If anyone desires to come after Me, let him deny himself, and take up his cross daily, and follow Me. For whoever desires to save his life will lose it, but whoever loses his life for My sake will save it.* (Luke 9:23-24)

In recent years, much of the doctrine of the Christian church has been man centered and not God centered. The concept of grace is a good example. Do you like the message of grace because it makes you feel better about yourself or do you like the message of grace because it gives you greater access to God? Do you like the message of faith because of what it will purchase for you or because of what its potential is for the kingdom of God? With that in mind, let's consider this important Scripture from Romans chapter 8.

> *There is therefore now no condemnation to those who are in Christ Jesus, who do not walk according to the flesh, but according to the Spirit. For the law of the Spirit of life in Christ Jesus has made me free from the law of sin and death.* (Romans 8:1-2)

The new covenant has released us from the burden of condemnation. The blood of Jesus Christ gives me access to the inner court of God's presence without the burden of shame or guilt. However, it must be clear our motivation is not fleshly but spiritual. If our goal is God, then we have nothing to hold us back. If our goal is to feel good about ourselves or to pursue our self-centered motivations, then we are not worthy of the law of the spirit.

Our natural and human desire is to take what we have done and preserve it for the future. Often this is motivated to provide an inheritance for our children or to preserve the glory of our contribution. Sometimes it will involve our desire to preserve the glory of someone else's accomplishments. We often want to honor people by building memorials to them; but we must always remember the church is a memorial to only one person, Jesus Christ. Jesus Christ has died for the church, and He is building the church. We are called to be living stones being built up as a holy habitation offering up sacrifices to God. What God is building is not for the glory of man but the glory of God.

> *you also, as living stones, are being built up a spiritual house, a holy priesthood, to offer up spiritual sacrifices acceptable to God through Jesus Christ.* (1 Peter 2:5)

The law of the spirit has replaced the law of Moses for those who are motivated to live for God. This motivation takes us into the walk of the spirit which makes us free from the law of sin and death. The problem with the people of God in the Old Testament was not their desire to serve the law of God. The prophets continually exhorted them to follow the law. The problem was they sought to follow the law from the flesh rather than by the power of the Spirit of God.

> *For what the law could not do in that it was weak through the flesh, God did by sending His own Son in the likeness of sinful flesh, on account of sin: He condemned sin in the flesh, that the righteous requirement of the law might be fulfilled in us who do not walk according to the flesh but according to the Spirit.* (Romans 8:3-4)

A God centered life will depend on the strength of God not the strength of man. The righteous requirements of the law could only be satisfied by the sacrifice of God. Human sacrifice is not a worthy substitute. The spiritually motivated person must set their mind and motivations on the things of the Spirit of God. Any other

205

motivation will bring death no matter how spiritual the goals or outcomes.

> *For those who live according to the flesh set their minds on the things of the flesh, but those who live according to the Spirit, the things of the Spirit. For to be carnally minded is death, but to be spiritually minded is life and peace. Because the carnal mind is enmity against God; for it is not subject to the law of God, nor indeed can be. So then, those who are in the flesh cannot please God.* (Romans 8:5-8)

When Jesus Christ came to the earth, there wasn't a lack of keepers of the law, there was a lack of keeping the law through faith in God. The end result of simply keeping the law as our motivation will be external and not of the heart. It will produce self-righteousness and will not satisfy the demands of God.

> *Woe to you, scribes and Pharisees, hypocrites! For you cleanse the outside of the cup and dish, but inside they are full of extortion and self-indulgence. Blind Pharisee, first cleanse the inside of the cup and dish, that the outside of them may be clean also. "Woe to you, scribes and Pharisees, hypocrites! For you are like whitewashed tombs which indeed appear beautiful outwardly, but inside are full of dead men's bones and all uncleanness. Even so you also outwardly appear righteous to men, but inside you are full of hypocrisy and lawlessness.* (Matthew 23:25-28)

It should be noted what defines spiritual versus what is carnal. Spiritual matters originate in the heart of man not the spirit of man. Many in our contemporary world claim to be followers of spiritual things. These so called spiritual things are things emotional or ethereal. Spiritual perception, according to Jesus Christ, is about the heart.

> *And in them the prophecy of Isaiah is fulfilled, which says: 'Hearing you will hear and shall not understand, And see-*

ing you will see and not perceive; For the hearts of this people have grown dull. Their ears are hard of hearing, And their eyes they have closed, Lest they should see with their eyes and hear with their ears, Lest they should understand with their hearts and turn, So that I should heal them. (Matthew 13:14-15)

The prophecy of Isaiah Jesus is referring to says, *"They honor me with their lips, but their heart is far from me."* A spiritually motivated person has set their heart and mind on the things of God. When God is your motivation, you may be influenced or swayed by your fleshly desires but you will deal with it once you see the difference. Since God has created us as triune beings, it is only logical we will be influenced by our body, soul, and spirit; but our heart must always belong to God. When God has your heart, He has you!

Therefore, brethren, we are debtors — not to the flesh, to live according to the flesh. For if you live according to the flesh you will die; but if by the Spirit you put to death the deeds of the body, you will live. For as many as are led by the Spirit of God, these are sons of God. (Romans 8:12-14)

Once liberated from the law of sin and death, we can find our comfort in knowing who we are in Christ Jesus. When we receive the Spirit of Christ, we have the Spirit of the Son. This spirit cries out to God as our Father. We are not slaves, but we are the children of the Most High God. God is our Father! He is also our "Abba" or daddy. We do not serve Him in fear but honor Him in love. With the blood of Jesus Christ as our covering, and with the confirmation of the Spirit of Christ, we can move forward in complete confidence that we will reach the divine destiny our Father has set before us. We have an inheritance bestowed upon us through Jesus Christ, and now it is time we walk as full heir sons of God in the earth.

And we know that all things work together for good to those who love God, to those who are the called according to His purpose. For whom He foreknew, He also predestined to be

conformed to the image of His Son, that He might be the
firstborn among many brethren. Moreover whom He predestined, these He also called; whom He called, these He also
justified; and whom He justified, these He also glorified. (Romans 8:28-30)

In the sense of our calling to be the sons of God, we are already glorified. What greater glory than to be called the son of God?
Yet, we also understand the glory of God is meant to be demonstrated through us in such a way that the people of the world will
see it.

For you did not receive the spirit of bondage again to fear,
but you received the Spirit of adoption by whom we cry out,
"Abba, Father." The Spirit Himself bears witness with our
spirit that we are children of God, and if children, then heirs
— heirs of God and joint heirs with Christ, if indeed we suffer with Him, that we may also be glorified together. (Romans 8:15-17)

It is time for the full glory of God to be received by the sons
of God. There is a condition here. What does it mean "if we suffer
with Him"? It should be obvious from the life of Jesus Christ that
the sons of God must live a life directed by the Father. Jesus Christ
had to make a choice to follow the will of the Father even though
it was unpleasant for Him. It should also be obvious that throughout history many of the greatest leaders in the body of Christ have
had to make tremendous sacrifice to fulfill their purpose. In order
to accomplish the purpose of the kingdom of God, sacrifices must
be made. These sacrifices represent the suffering in the flesh that
will reveal the sons of God in the earth.

For Jesus Christ, His choice made in the garden of Gethsemane was to accept the responsibility of the cross. Nothing would
have been possible without the sacrifice He made. It was a sacrifice
He made at tremendous personal cost. He had to be willing to give
His life. Many people in church history have had to literally give up

their lives for the sake of the kingdom of God. We usually are not literally required to die as martyrs, but we must love the life God has for us more than we love life itself. It will be this attitude that will destroy the power of the enemy and fully establish the kingdom of God in the earth.

> *Then I heard a loud voice saying in heaven, "Now salvation, and strength, and the kingdom of our God, and the power of His Christ have come, for the accuser of our brethren, who accused them before our God day and night, has been cast down. And they overcame him by the blood of the Lamb and by the word of their testimony, and they did not love their lives to the death.* (Revelation 12:10-11)

I know for the average Christian this concept seems far fetched. Our expectations when it comes to human behavior are not high. Most of our philosophy is built on the idea that God's grace is the only way we can be pleasing to God. This is absolutely right. Yet, we must understand God's grace is not just His mercy but also His empowerment. With man these ideas seem impossible, but with God all things are possible. When we see God's hand at work through eternity, I believe we can see how the possibilities are increasing. When we look at the behavior of people in the days of Moses, we can understand why the law was necessary for the time. Most people see the law as only a restriction on behavior to make them pleasing to God. When we really see the law in the context of the time, it is clear God had His people in mind. This is why the people in the past had a hard time receiving the ministry of Jesus Christ. They did not understand God's laws were **for** man not against him.

> *And He said to them, "The Sabbath was made for man, and not man for the Sabbath. Therefore the Son of Man is also Lord of the Sabbath."* (Mark 2:27-28)

It is obvious to me, from the Scriptures and from my personal experience, that God is for us. God is not against His creation. God is not against man.

It is a good thing God is bringing us past the stage of legalism that has bound up the church for many years. Yet, our freedom from legalism should not set us on the course of a self-centered life. We should now approach our Christian experience as full heir sons of God who always consider the wisdom and the Word of God as the course for our lives with the full intent of making our lives pleasing to God. We are not as children who need constant oversight, but we should be mature enough to hear the voice within telling us the difference between the right course and the wrong one. Our teachers are not constant in their oversight, but our eyes see the right course because our teachers have taught us the way of life.

> *And though the Lord gives you The bread of adversity and the water of affliction, Yet your teachers will not be moved into a corner anymore, But your eyes shall see your teachers. Your ears shall hear a word behind you, saying, "This is the way, walk in it," Whenever you turn to the right hand Or whenever you turn to the left.* (Isaiah 30:20-21)

As the mature sons of God, we will have submitted ourselves to instruction both through the body and through the hand of God. This can only come through the church that is truly the family of God: God, the Father of the family; the church, our mother; and us, as the children of our heavenly Father. Many Christians hold to the comfort of their mother but never allow the Father to take His place as their instructor. We can only become sons when we give ourselves to the instruction of the Father.

> *If you endure chastening, God deals with you as with sons; for what son is there whom a father does not chasten? But if you are without chastening, of which all have become partakers, then you are illegitimate and not sons. Furthermore, we have had human fathers who corrected us, and we paid them re-*

210

spect. Shall we not much more readily be in subjection to the Father of spirits and live? (Hebrews 12:7-9)

To facilitate this change, the leaders of the church need to see their proper place in bringing the people of God to maturity. Our goal should not be to develop perpetual children always in need to the parenting of the mother. Like in the natural, our goal should be to bring people to the place of fellowship with God and the church from a position of maturity. This will only be possible when we have true spiritual fathers taking their place of leadership in the church. This is the role of the apostolic ministry of the church. The apostle Paul stressed to the Corinthian church their need for fathers. He was their father, and he encouraged them to follow the example he had set before them.

I do not write these things to shame you, but as my beloved children I warn you. For though you might have ten thousand instructors in Christ, yet you do not have many fathers; for in Christ Jesus I have begotten you through the gospel. Therefore I urge you, imitate me. (1 Corinthians 4:14-16)

We have seen a recent emphasis on the ministry of the apostle, but there has been very little understanding how the concept fits into the structure of the church. The apostle Paul was bold enough to declare that the church should look to him as an example. In order for this concept to work, we need church fathers who commit themselves to the responsibility of being an example. We need responsible ministers who will be examples that will inspire others to greatness in God. The example of the Father was the motivation for the ministry of Jesus Christ. He declared how necessary it is for fathers to be an example to their sons.

Then Jesus answered and said to them, "Most assuredly, I say to you, the Son can do nothing of Himself, but what He sees the Father do; for whatever He does, the Son also does in like manner. (John 5:19)

211

The restoration of the ministry and function of the father will be a major aspect of the last day move of God. The restoration of the father to the sons is the ministry of Elijah that will release the ministry of the sons of God in the earth.

> *Behold, I will send you Elijah the prophet Before the coming of the great and dreadful day of the LORD. And he will turn The hearts of the fathers to the children, And the hearts of the children to their fathers, Lest I come and strike the earth with a curse.* (Malachi 4:5-6)

Although this is important to the nuclear family, we must understand that from the beginning, the family unit and marriage are a picture of God's desire for His church. We cannot put all the families of the earth back together nor will we be able to create a substitute for the lack of fathers within the family, but the church can make up the difference and make all of us vital members of the family of God.

Church structure is another aspect, but what we want to inspire in this book is the idea we can and will be what the Father has called us to be. More than anything, it is about the pursuit of our goal in our walk with God. God has placed all His plans on us. Even the creation groans for the revealing of the sons of God in the earth.

> *For the earnest expectation of the creation eagerly waits for the revealing of the sons of God. For the creation was subjected to futility, not willingly, but because of Him who subjected it in hope; because the creation itself also will be delivered from the bondage of corruption into the glorious liberty of the children of God.* (Romans 8:19-21)

Note, the subjection of creation to the purpose of God for man was not the result of the fall of man but was God's original intent. Many people see the world in disorder because of the fall of man, but the Scripture tells us God created everything to wait in expectation of man. He created man to take dominion of His creation; and until man fulfills his destiny, the natural order will be in

212

the futility of what is called the circle of life. This circle is built on the premise of the dog eat dog, predator eat prey world. The Scripture is clear God created the world in need of the stewardship of man.

We are living in a day when the whole of creation is in birth pangs. The signs of this labor are in the natural realm and in the realm of man. This groaning, in the end, will bring forth the birth of the sons of God.

> *For we know that the whole creation groans and labors with birth pangs together until now. Not only that, but we also who have the firstfruits of the Spirit, even we ourselves groan within ourselves, eagerly waiting for the adoption, the redemption of our body. For we were saved in this hope, but hope that is seen is not hope; for why does one still hope for what he sees? But if we hope for what we do not see, we eagerly wait for it with perseverance.* (Romans 8:22-25)

This groan is also in each and every one of us. Do you feel the groan inside of you? Ever since I was called of God as a teenager, I have felt the groan of God and the call to my eternal purpose leading me to the higher place God has for me. I know many of the people of God have been called for such a time as this, and the time of God is at hand. It is time for us to see and take our place. With new hope and expectation, we must set ourselves in the direction God has for us. I want the hope God has for me. You and I have been chosen for God's eternal purpose. This choosing resulted in the call of God and the work of God inside of you. You need to see how God has directed all things in your life for His purpose knowing the glory that awaits you!

> *For it was fitting for Him, for whom are all things and by whom are all things, in bringing many sons to glory, to make the captain of their salvation perfect through sufferings. For both He who sanctifies and those who are being sanctified are*

all of one, for which reason He is not ashamed to call them brethren, (Hebrews 2:10-11)

From the beginning, God has desired to bring forth His sons. He created all men with the potential to become the sons of God in the earth. The fullness of this potential would only come in time as God prepared man to receive His plan. As we have learned concerning the divine process, it began in the natural when He created Adam and Eve in the beginning. The second part would only be possible when the last Adam, Jesus Christ, came to impart the Life-Giving Spirit to us. Just as God waited for mankind as a whole, we have seen Him patiently wait over time for the church to grow and develop. Notice this Scripture in Hebrews declares of God that, "all things are for Him and all things are from Him." When you see God for who He is, you will never doubt that all His intentions for earth and for man will be fulfilled. It is only a matter of time. We have watched the patience of God allow for all the time He needs. We need to be more mindful of His process while we take our place as His true sons in the earth.

> *And we know that all things work together for good to those who love God, to those who are the called according to His purpose. For whom He foreknew, He also predestined to be conformed to the image of His Son, that He might be the firstborn among many brethren. Moreover whom He predestined, these He also called; whom He called, these He also justified; and whom He justified, these He also glorified.* (Romans 8:28-30)

In Summary

God's plan is for us to become the sons of God in the earth. As the sons of God, we will bear the image of God and fulfill the Father's purpose in the earth. A hindrance to our fulfilling God's plan is when we become man centered rather than God centered. When our course involves the pursuit of a self-centered motivation, it will bring death no matter how sincere the motives may appear. It must be clear our motivation is not fleshly but spiritual. We are called to be living stones being built up as a holy habitation offering up sacrifices to God. What God is building is not for the glory of man but the glory of God.

When Jesus Christ came to the earth, there wasn't a lack of keepers of the law; rather there was a lack of keeping the law through faith in God. The end result of simply keeping the law as our motivation will be external and not of the heart. It will produce self-righteousness and will not satisfy the demands of God.

In order to accomplish the purpose of the kingdom of God, sacrifices must be made. These sacrifices represent the suffering in the flesh that will reveal the sons of God in the earth. Most of our philosophy is built on the idea that God's grace is the only way we can be pleasing to God. Yet, we must understand God's grace is not just His mercy but also His empowerment. God's grace gives us the power to become His son. God's grace frees us from legalism by giving us understanding that as a mature son, who loves God and wants to please Him, we can develop the ability to hear the voice of God within us telling us what is right and what is wrong. As full heir sons of God, we should then approach our Christian experience considering the wisdom and the Word of God as the course for our lives with the full intent of making our lives pleasing to Him. To arrive at this place, we need fathers that will correct and instruct us. We need fathers to take a place of leadership and become examples in the church. The restoration of the ministry and function of the father will be a major aspect of the last day move of God.

Chapter Fifteen

Did You Know God Wants to Bring You to a Place of Glory?

For it was fitting for Him, for whom are all things and by whom are all things, in bringing many sons to glory, to make the captain of their salvation perfect through sufferings. For both He who sanctifies and those who are being sanctified are all of one, for which reason He is not ashamed to call them brethren, (Hebrews 2:10-11)

God is bringing us to glory! Isn't it amazing the wonderful things God has planned for His people? As we have mentioned before, His eternal purpose involves bringing us into a place of being conformed to the image of God. This is a process that begins with being chosen by God; then being justified, or put in right standing with God; but ultimately, being glorified together with Christ. The exciting thing about God is He does desire to share His glory with us. We are called to bask in and to demonstrate to the world the glory of God. God has enough glory to pass around, but we need to see ourselves as sharing His glory, not trying to create or boast in a glory of our own. Our glory is the fact we are chosen to be the sons of God in the earth. This has been the eternal purpose of God for you from the beginning.

The Spirit Himself bears witness with our spirit that we are children of God, and if children, then heirs — heirs of God and joint heirs with Christ, if indeed we suffer with Him, that we may also be glorified together. (Romans 8:16-17)

The author of our salvation was made perfect through suffering, and we must acknowledge that suffering with Him will bring us to the place of sharing His glory.

The glory of God is an important concept to understand. What is the glory of God? Actually, it is everything about Him that makes Him who He is. His glory gives us reason to give Him praise. His glory speaks of His abundance, wealth, and treasures; hence, all the honor His abundance gives to Him. Moses was a man who desired to see God's glory. When he requested to see the glory of God, the Lord told him he was asking for something hard. There is a part of the glory of God he could not see and still live. Because of his love and sincerity, God did allow Moses to get a glimpse of His glory. He told Moses he would have to stand behind a rock to shield himself, and from that vantage point he could see God's backside. Moses got a glimpse of the emanating glory of God. God's emanating glory is a force so powerful one would need protection from it. It is interesting what Moses saw but more importantly what he heard through his experience.

> *Then He said, "I will make all My goodness pass before you, and I will proclaim the name of the LORD before you. I will be gracious to whom I will be gracious, and I will have compassion on whom I will have compassion." (Exodus 33:19)*

Moses saw the pattern of God's revelation concerning Himself that we would not see until the New Testament. Jesus declared how this revelation of God works.

> *No one has seen God at any time. The only begotten Son, who is in the bosom of the Father, He has declared Him. (John 1:18)*

The person of God includes the Father. He is the ultimate expression of the Godhead who has no visible form that we could comprehend and relate to. Jesus Christ was the visible image of the invisible God. He came as the visible expression of God and as the

218

Word or voice of God to man. Moses had a picture of this same experience.

> Now the LORD descended in the cloud and stood with him there, and proclaimed the name of the LORD. And the LORD passed before him and proclaimed, "The LORD, the LORD God, merciful and gracious, longsuffering, and abounding in goodness and truth, keeping mercy for thousands, forgiving iniquity and transgression and sin, by no means clearing the guilty, visiting the iniquity of the fathers upon the children and the children's children to the third and the fourth generation." (Exodus 34:5-7)

The exposure to the glory of God actually emanated on Moses' face when he came down from the mountain to talk to the children of Israel. How amazing that would have been to be in the presence of God and have the glory of the light of God shine on us! Although it was an amazing concept, it should not be the aspiration of a New Testament believer. God has something better for us.

> But if the ministry of death, written and engraved on stones, was glorious, so that the children of Israel could not look steadily at the face of Moses because of the glory of his countenance, which glory was passing away, how will the ministry of the Spirit not be more glorious? For if the ministry of condemnation had glory, the ministry of righteousness exceeds much more in glory. For even what was made glorious had no glory in this respect, because of the glory that excels. For if what is passing away was glorious, what remains is much more glorious. (2 Corinthians 3:7-11)

The glory Moses revealed was like the covenant he instituted; it was something temporary. The greater glory Moses encountered was the glory of who God was. God is a God of justice; but He is also a God of mercy, grace, and goodness. God's character and person is the greater part of His glory, and it is this glory Jesus Christ came to reveal to us and give us the opportunity to share.

And the Word became flesh and dwelt among us, and we be-held His glory, the glory as of the only begotten of the Father, full of grace and truth And of His fullness we have all re-ceived, and grace for grace. For the law was given through Moses, but grace and truth came through Jesus Christ. No one has seen God at any time. The only begotten Son, who is in the bosom of the Father, He has declared Him. (John 1:14, 16-18)

Now, the goal of the sons of God is to have a heart to pursue God as the patriarchs before us and to allow the glory of who He is to shine on and through us.

Now the Lord is the Spirit; and where the Spirit of the Lord is, there is liberty. But we all, with unveiled face, beholding as in a mirror the glory of the Lord, are being transformed into the same image from glory to glory, just as by the Spirit of the Lord. (2 Corinthians 3:17-18)

In the beginning, when God created man, He created us in His image and His likeness. From this perspective, Jesus Christ is our example for He was the image of God. Since Jesus came to show us what God would be like as a man, we should strive not to be God but to be godly people. Often in contemplating the glory of God, we are more inclined to desire to see and demonstrate the "glitter glory" Moses saw rather than the glory of the person of God. The glory that glittered on Moses was something on him but not a part of him. The New Testament pattern is to make the glory a part of us so we can be a part of the glory. This glory manifests it-self through us as we allow God to write it on the fleshly tables of our heart rather than it being something external like the Old Tes-tament pattern.

clearly you are an epistle of Christ, ministered by us, written not with ink but by the Spirit of the living God, not on tablets of stone but on tablets of flesh, that is, of the heart. (2 Corinthians 3:3)

This is why the revelation of God's glory through us will have some suffering connected with it. Letting God write on the "fleshly tablet" of the heart can be painful. Our heart represents everything about our desires. Sometimes our desires conflict with God's eternal purpose. When this happens, we must give God our heart and let Him write upon it. This is what happened to Jesus Christ. Like Jesus Christ before us, we must deny our will and submit to the Father's purpose even when we don't like what we have to experience. Jesus showed us the way when in the garden of Gethsemane He said, "Father not My will but Yours be done." Our will is connected to our desires. If God's will conflicts, we must fully surrender our desire to Him. There can be loss on this path. Loss is not easy to bear. Jesus Christ told His disciples about this process but also assured them there would be no loss God would not redeem. He is not the God of loss but the God of gain. What we gain from Him could cost us something in the process. We must keep ourselves focused on the gain.

> So Jesus answered and said, "Assuredly, I say to you, there is no one who has left house or brothers or sisters or father or mother or wife or children or lands, for My sake and the gospel's, who shall not receive a hundredfold now in this time — houses and brothers and sisters and mothers and children and lands, with persecutions — and in the age to come, eternal life. (Mark 10:29-30)

It means, like Jesus, our personal life will have experiences we don't want in order to prepare us to minister to the needs of others. Jesus had compassion, which literally means to feel someone's pain. How does this happen? We often have to experience those pains so we have a reservoir of feelings to draw on. Sometimes it is from our present tense pain we have an opportunity to minister to others. As we receive the strength we need, it becomes a resource we have to give to others.

> *Blessed be the God and Father of our Lord Jesus Christ, the Father of mercies and God of all comfort, who comforts us in all our tribulation, that we may be able to comfort those who are in any trouble, with the comfort with which we ourselves are comforted by God.* (2 Corinthians 1:3-4)

The Scriptures tell us Jesus Christ was a man of sorrows who was acquainted with grief. This could have been His temperament. Sometimes we have a temperament that will cause us certain emotions or feelings. If they are sad feelings, our human response is to rid ourselves of them. Who would want to feel sad? Well, some of the greatest contributors to human civilization were people with this temperament. Like Jesus Christ, we may have a temperament we would rather not have but that we are willing to accept in order to fulfill the purpose of our Father. Jesus Christ, as a man of sorrows; obviously, had a temperament that would have caused Him pain. Many times as Christians, we seek for God to change the things about ourselves we do not like when the Father's purpose would be better suited for us to be the way we are. Perhaps, for God's purpose, we may need to "temper" our temperament so He can use it for His glory.

The Scriptures tell us in Hebrews chapter 1 that Jesus Christ, who is the author of our salvation, will bring many sons to glory. It is fitting that it says He would do so through suffering. There is a cost to get where God wants to take us. The cost comes in the flesh. The suffering is the result of denying our natural realm to bring forth the spiritual one. As it was for the author, so it must be for us.

> *Therefore, since Christ suffered for us in the flesh, arm yourselves also with the same mind, for he who has suffered in the flesh has ceased from sin, that he no longer should live the rest of his time in the flesh for the lusts of men, but for the will of God.* (1 Peter 4:1-2)

Jesus was made perfect through suffering. This is a very important concept to understand. I have heard many Christians over the years say, "Christians aren't perfect; we're just forgiven." This statement is meant to give grace to the faults we have so we do not come under the judgment of others. The problem is we corrupt the plan of God. God **has** called us to perfection. The word perfection in this case does not mean we are without flaws. It means we have reached our destiny. Jesus Christ was clearly the "unblemished" and "unspotted" Lamb of God. Yet, the Scripture says He had to be perfected. It was only in His perfection He could be the author of our salvation.

> who, in the days of His flesh, when He had offered up prayers and supplications, with vehement cries and tears to Him who was able to save Him from death, and was heard because of His godly fear, though He was a Son, yet He learned obedience by the things which He suffered. And having been perfected, He became the author of eternal salvation to all who obey Him, (Hebrews 5:7-9)

Jesus' perfection was tied to His willingness to give Himself to the purpose of the Father, even when it was something totally against Him. As a man, Jesus showed us that even the perfect Lamb would resist the suffering of His person. His purpose was settled in the garden of Gethsemane. The purpose started in a garden, and now the ultimate power would come in a garden. Jesus was overwhelmed by human emotions in the garden. The issue with God is not how we feel but what we choose. He chose to follow the purpose of the Father because of "godly fear." Fear is the beginning of wisdom, and we should never lose the fear of the Lord. Notice it says here, "He was heard." Being heard by God does not mean you get what you want. It means God heard the prayer built on what He wants. Our prayers must line up with the will of God. What was the answer He received? The answer He received from God was the grace of empowerment. Heaven opened to Him, and He was strengthened.

saying, "Father, if it is Your will, take this cup away from Me; nevertheless not My will, but Yours, be done." Then an angel appeared to Him from heaven, strengthening Him. (Luke 22:42-43)

Now is the time for the church to begin to hear the call of God to go on to maturity. It is time for us to no longer be children but the mature sons of God. We have lived on milk long enough. Now it is time for solid food.

For though by this time you ought to be teachers, you need someone to teach you again the first principles of the oracles of God; and you have come to need milk and not solid food. For everyone who partakes only of milk is unskilled in the word of righteousness, for he is a babe. But solid food belongs to those who are of full age, that is, those who by reason of use have their senses exercised to discern both good and evil. (Hebrews 5:12-14)

When thinking about the glory of God, it is so easy to see the glory of the past and not see the glory of the present. Growing up in church, I often heard people talk about the "good ole days." This was especially true in Pentecostal charismatic circles. Of course, they always pointed back to the book of Acts and the early church as the glory days we should strive to attain. We need to hear the prophetic voice God raised up for the house of Israel when they were rebuilding the temple, after their return from captivity in Babylon. When the people saw what God was doing in their day, all they could think about was the past. The shouts of excitement were drowned out by the cries of the people who remembered the former glory. It took the voice of the prophets to point to the future and get the people to see God was the God of the future and not just the past. They needed to understand the greater glory was yet to come.

"For thus says the LORD of hosts: 'Once more (it is a little while) I will shake heaven and earth, the sea and dry land;

and I will shake all nations, and they shall come to the Desire of All Nations, and I will fill this temple with glory,' says the LORD of hosts. 'The silver is Mine, and the gold is Mine,' says the LORD of hosts. 'The glory of this latter temple shall be greater than the former,' says the LORD of hosts. 'And in this place I will give peace,' says the LORD of hosts." (Haggai 2:6-9)

There is more to salvation than having the right formula for going to heaven. The book of Hebrews is a book urging us to go forth and showing us the way. We will not go forward if we just concern ourselves with the first principles.

Therefore, leaving the discussion of the elementary principles of Christ, let us go on to perfection, not laying again the foundation of repentance from dead works and of faith toward God, of the doctrine of baptisms, of laying on of hands, of resurrection of the dead, and of eternal judgment. And this we will do if God permits. (Hebrews 6:1-3)

The "if" in verse 3, is very important. Although the author of this book of the Bible knows the plan, he did not know the timing. The permit to go on to perfection was not given in the past, but I sense it is being given to us in this time. It is time to go on to maturity and become all the Father has planned us to be. With God, the timing is everything. When it is not the time, it is not possible. When Jesus Christ came, people were required to receive the message of the time; but they could not have fully appreciated how to relate this to the whole story of God that started in the beginning. God, in His mercy and patience, gave us a long time to figure out the relationship between the Father, Son, and Holy Spirit. This comprehension took time and God gave it. This is why it is so important to understand God's appointed times and the beauty of that time, even when we fail to understand it in its fullness.

To everything there is a season, A time for every purpose under heaven: I have seen the God-given task with which the sons of men are to be occupied. He has made everything beautiful in its time. Also He has put eternity in their hearts, except that no one can find out the work that God does from beginning to end. (Ecclesiastes 3:1, 10-11)

Although we know everything is beautiful in its time, we need to be careful not to allow our rejoicing in the time to keep us locked into the time. God's plan is progressive, and we need to enjoy the time with an eye and heart to the future. As we have learned how important it is to tap into the eternity our hearts long for, we also need to flow with the eternal plan. We must recognize we cannot stay still or glory in the past, but we must always press forward to what God has in store for us. The eternal God is building something. We must be careful not to build our buildings and organizations around what He is building, hoping to hold it in place to protect our investment. God's purpose involves us, but God usually has to get us out of the way in order to add what He is doing. After we name and organize the work of God, we typically want to preserve it for future generations rather than allow those generations to build on what we have done. God certainly wants us to be able to understand the past but not live in it. When we see the progressive plan of God, we will seek to learn how to take what God has already done and allow Him to build on it.

I know that nothing is better for them than to rejoice, and to do good in their lives, and also that every man should eat and drink and enjoy the good of all his labor — it is the gift of God. I know that whatever God does, It shall be forever. Nothing can be added to it, And nothing taken from it. God does it, that men should fear before Him. (Ecclesiastes 3:12-14)

When it is not the time, God does not judge us according to the seasons of the future. Like a good Father, His expectations are built on the times of life and development. But there does come the time when God calls us to a higher plane, and we must respond. This process of development was aptly demonstrated in the father of our faith, Abraham. When the appointed time came, God raised the bar of expectation for him.

> *When Abram was ninety-nine years old, the LORD appeared to Abram and said to him, "I am Almighty God; walk before Me and be blameless (Perfect). And I will make My covenant between Me and you, and will multiply you exceedingly."* (Genesis 17:1-2)

I added the word "perfect" to this NKJ version because it is the word that corresponds to the word "perfect" in the New Testament. It is translated as perfect in the KJV and many other texts. Using the word "blameless" gives the impression of the word "unblemished" and certainly describes the one and only begotten Son of God, Jesus Christ. It is important to note the command is built on the revelation of God. When you know God is the Almighty, you will not argue with Him about the potential you or anybody else has. Abraham and his wife Sarah, at this time, would move beyond the scope of their human ability to the supernatural power of God. God is calling us to that level today, and we must be ready and willing to take the higher step. Like Abraham, we need faith and patience; but we also need to see the hope we have in God to fulfill all things He has promised us. God doesn't lie. He makes covenant commitments He will not break.

> *For when God made a promise to Abraham, because He could swear by no one greater, He swore by Himself, saying, "Surely blessing I will bless you, and multiplying I will multiply you." And so, after he had patiently endured, he obtained the promise. For men indeed swear by the greater, and an oath for confirmation is for them an end of all dispute. Thus God, determining to show more abundantly to the heirs of promise the immutability of His counsel, confirmed it by an oath, that by two immutable things, in which it is impossible for God to lie, we might have strong consolation, who have*

227

fled for refuge to lay hold of the hope set before us. (Hebrews 6:13-18)

The oath God has made with us is the oath He pledged concerning the new covenant. The new covenant would not rely on the strength of man but the strength of God. This strength would be given to us by God, impacting and empowering us from the inside, so we could be all God has purposed us to be to manifest His glory to the nations.

> *But the Holy Spirit also witnesses to us; for after He had said before, "This is the covenant that I will make with them after those days, says the LORD: I will put My laws into their hearts, and in their minds I will write them," then He adds, "Their sins and their lawless deeds I will remember no more." Now where there is remission of these, there is no longer an offering for sin.* (Hebrews 10:15-18)

We should not approach this covenant promise in a passive way but in an aggressive manner. We shouldn't just look for what God will do for us, but we should understand we are called as His sons to do something for Him. We need to remind ourselves of the blessings of our past and then with confidence push forward to the future we have with God. As children, our promises were all about us; but as the sons of God, we need to embrace the promised purpose of God and fulfill our place in the eternal purpose of God!

> *But recall the former days in which, after you were illuminated, you endured a great struggle with sufferings: Therefore do not cast away your confidence, which has great reward. For you have need of endurance, so that after you have done the will of God, you may receive the promise:* (Hebrews 10:32, 35-36)

Hebrews chapter 10 continues with the exhortation of chapter 6. We must, through "faith and patience," inherit the promises of God. This path to perfection involves the development of our character and involves a mature understanding of God's plan and purpose. Abraham could not have inherited the blessing he received from God through faith alone. His journey was thirty years to the birth of his son and seventeen more years until the full appropriation of the blessing pronounced upon him when He offered Isaac upon the altar at Mount Moriah.

> and said: "By Myself I have sworn, says the LORD, because you have done this thing, and have not withheld your son, your only son — blessing I will bless you, and multiplying I will multiply your descendants as the stars of the heaven and as the sand which is on the seashore; and your descendants shall possess the gate of their enemies. In your seed all the nations of the earth shall be blessed, because you have obeyed My voice." (Genesis 22:16-18)

This represents the ultimate blessing. Abraham was willing to do what God asked of him and in return God declared that He would bless Abraham for his faithfulness to the plan of God. Abraham contributed to God's eternal plan for the ages, the plan of God that is from the beginning and for eternity.

Truly, Abraham became "perfected" or complete that day on the mountain when he was willing to give his only son, Isaac, to God. Abraham showed himself to be like his heavenly Father who was willing to lay down the life of His only Son for the sins of the world. Such faith to bring glory to God is amazing, yet, it did not come from Abraham's confidence in himself. It came from his faith in Jehovah Jirah, the God who provides.

> And Abraham called the name of the place, The-LORD-Will-Provide; as it is said to this day, "In the Mount of the LORD it shall be provided." (Genesis 22:14)

The early apostles, like Jesus Christ, died to form the foundation of the church that will one day be everything God has called it to be. The church will be glorious as Jesus puts the finishing touches on it in these latter days of time. When Jesus Christ is done, the glory of God will emanate and the nations of the world will see it.

> *Now it shall come to pass in the latter days That the moun-*
> *tain of the LORD's house Shall be established on the top of*
> *the mountains, And shall be exalted above the hills; And all*
> *nations shall flow to it. Many people shall come and say,*
> *"Come, and let us go up to the mountain of the LORD, To the*
> *house of the God of Jacob; He will teach us His ways, And we*
> *shall walk in His paths." For out of Zion shall go forth the law,*
> *And the word of the LORD from Jerusalem.* (Isaiah 2:2-3)

The Scriptures declare we are the glory of God.

> *For a man indeed ought not to cover his head, since he is the*
> *image and glory of God . . .* (1 Corinthians 11:7)

I do not want to discuss the context of these Scriptures; I simply want to point out that we are indeed the glory of God. We are in the process of becoming all we are meant to be. We are not there yet, but we are assured in the Scriptures that we will be when He returns to the earth.

> *Beloved, now we are children of God; and it has not yet been*
> *revealed what we shall be, but we know that when He is re-*
> *vealed, we shall be like Him, for we shall see Him as He is.*
> *And everyone who has this hope in Him purifies himself, just*
> *as He is pure.* (1 John 3:2-3)

When the children of Israel refused to accept the challenge to go into the Promised Land, God told Moses He would disinherit them and raise up the seed of Moses to take their place. You can tell from that statement that God is not in a hurry and does not want to settle for second best. Moses cried out to God for His mercy. God granted his request and then made a strong affirmation of His intent.

Then the LORD said: "I have pardoned, according to your word; but truly, as I live, all the earth shall be filled with the glory of the LORD — (Numbers 14:20-21)

We are living in the time when God wants to lift our vision higher. He doesn't want us to settle for a lower place because our faith is not big enough or we don't see ourselves as strong enough. We will not be able to lift our vision higher without a change in our thinking. It is time to get God's mind and heart and to understand His purpose for the earth. It is time to yield with confidence to His plan for man!

In Summary

God desires for us to share in His glory. Our glory is the fact we are chosen to be the sons of God in the earth. What is the glory of God? Actually, it is everything about Him that makes Him who He is. God's character and person is the greater part of His glory, and it is this glory Jesus Christ came to reveal to us and give us the opportunity to share.

The Scriptures tell us that Jesus was made perfect through suffering and we must acknowledge that suffering with Him will bring us to the place of sharing His glory. This glory manifests itself through us as we allow God to write it on the fleshly tables of our heart rather than it being something external like the Old Testament pattern. This is why the revelation of God's glory through us will have some suffering connected with it. Letting God write on the "fleshly tablet" of the heart can be painful. There is a cost to get where God wants to take us. The cost comes in the flesh. The suffering is the result of denying our natural realm to bring forth the spiritual one.

God has called us to perfection. The word "perfection" in this case does not mean we are without flaws. It means we have reached our destiny. Jesus suffered when He struggled with the plan of God for His life in the garden of Gethsemane. Jesus' perfection was tied to His willingness to give Himself to the purpose of the Father.

231

Jesus struggled with His emotions but He chose to follow the purpose of the Father. The issue with God is not how we feel but what we choose. Jesus prayed to the Father and the Father heard Him. The answer He received from God was the grace of empowerment. Heaven opened to Him, and He was strengthened. The oath God has made with us is the oath He pledged concerning the new covenant. The new covenant would not rely on the strength of man but the strength of God. This strength would be given to us by God, impacting and empowering us from the inside, so we could be all God has purposed us to be to manifest His glory to the nations.

The path to perfection involves the development of our character and involves a mature understanding of God's plan and purpose. It is not enough to have faith. We must exercise our faith to allow us to confidentially move forward in the path that God has for us, so that we accomplish His will in the earth. When we have obtained a place of perfection or completion, we will be able to represent God's glory to the world.

Conclusion

Let us therefore come boldly to the throne of grace, that we may obtain mercy and find grace to help in time of need. (Hebrews 4:16)

Under the old covenant, once a year, the high priest would enter the Most Holy Place. In the Most Holy Place, he would sprinkle blood on the mercy seat to make atonement for the people of God. On this holy day, the nation was cleansed from its sin so the people could face another year as the children of God. This pattern was repeated year after year on this day, for it was a holy day unto the Lord. The problem with this sacrifice, and all the other offerings made throughout the year, was that they did not take the people anywhere. The process would only grant a reprieve, making it necessary for them to go through the same process year after year. We have created a similar repeat process in the modern Christian church. People continually go over the same religious experiences without any understanding that the experiences are supposed to take them somewhere. Since we have made our end goal heaven, everything we do on earth is a religious pattern that causes us to simply "bide" our time. It is time for us to see God's eternal purpose so we can actually go somewhere in God. Instead of repeating the same patterns and arguments, we need to go on to perfection or completion in God.

Therefore, leaving the discussion of the elementary principles of Christ, let us go on to perfection, not laying again the foundation of repentance from dead works and of faith toward God, of the doctrine of baptisms, of laying on of hands, of resurrection of the dead, and of eternal judgment. And this we will do if God permits. (Hebrews 6:1-3)

We need to understand that the Old Testament order was not a pointless endeavor. It set the stage for the future plan God had for His people. The new plan, or covenant, would not just give us a reprieve but would actually take us to the place of completion or perfection God wanted for us. This would be the place where we would fulfill the Father's plan and the purpose He had for us in the beginning. The inferiority of the Old Testament, or covenant, does not discount its value when you realize it did accomplish its purpose.

> *Therefore, if perfection were through the Levitical priesthood (for under it the people received the law), what further need was there that another priest should rise according to the order of Melchizedek, and not be called according to the order of Aaron? For the priesthood being changed, of necessity there is also a change of the law.* (Hebrews 7:11-12)

When we realize God has an eternal plan, we need to learn the lesson of the current plan so we can move forward to the next level. God instituted the Old Testament plan to prepare us for the New Testament. It wasn't because the failure of the old plan made another plan necessary. God's plan from the beginning was to bring many sons to glory. It was a progressive plan with each level necessary for the next. When God was ready to make His presence fully available to all His people, He sent His Son, Jesus Christ, to once and for all make the perfect sacrifice that would make the most Holy Place of God's presence available to us. Once His blood was sprinkled on the heavenly mercy seat, not only was forgiveness granted but the goal was to take us from the place of sin consciousness to the place of being fully God conscious. The repetitious patterns of the Old Testament not only kept them walking in circles but it made them continually aware of their sinful condition.

> *But in those sacrifices there is a reminder of sins every year. For it is not possible that the blood of bulls and goats could take away sins.* (Hebrews 10:3-4)

In the new covenant, God not only takes away our sins but He wants to remove the sin consciousness that was a regular part of the old covenant.

For then would they not have ceased to be offered? For the worshipers, once purified, would have had no more consciousness of sins. (Hebrews 10:2)

Through the blood sacrifice of Jesus Christ, we are made clean and are perfected in our sanctification.

For by one offering He has perfected forever those who are being sanctified. But the Holy Spirit also witnesses to us; for after He had said before, "This is the covenant that I will make with them after those days, says the LORD: I will put My laws into their hearts, and in their minds I will write them," then He adds, "Their sins and their lawless deeds I will remember no more." Now where there is remission of these, there is no longer an offering for sin. (Hebrews 10:14-18)

It is at this point many Christians miss the understanding of God's eternal purpose. If God's eternal purpose was just to have fellowship with man, this would be our endpoint. We could preach the gospel of forgiveness and reconciliation to God, and our only concern would be to fill up heaven with people. Unfortunately, although this is a refreshing endpoint for people who love God's presence, it does not satisfy the Father's eternal plan or His desire for us. Clearly, God's desire is to have Jesus Christ as the pattern for many sons who will fulfill their Father's purpose in the earth.

For thus says the LORD, Who created the heavens, Who is God, Who formed the earth and made it, Who has established it, Who did not create it in vain, Who formed it to be inhabited: "I am the LORD, and there is no other. (Isaiah 45:18)

The earth was not created as a nursery to birth babies for heaven. The earth was created by God for a purpose and for a place of habitation. The earth was uniquely chosen as a place to reveal the glory of God, and mankind is the agent by which this purpose will be accomplished. Once we understand His purpose, we can fully understand His grace. God's grace has a two-fold purpose. The first purpose is to pour out God's mercy on us so we can be fully reconciled to God. Secondly, His grace is God enabling us to fulfill the divine purpose He has called us to. This is why our opening verse says: *"Let us therefore come boldly to the throne of grace, that we may obtain mercy and find grace to help in the time of need."* The first provision of grace is mercy. It represents God's unmerited favor toward the heirs of His great salvation. After mercy, God wants us to see His grace ultimately providing the help we need to fulfill the purpose He has for us. Even Jesus Christ Himself needed that grace in the garden of Gethsemane to fully apprehend the help needed to fulfill His horrendous call.

> *who, in the days of His flesh, when He had offered up prayers and supplications, with vehement cries and tears to Him who was able to save Him from death, and was heard because of His godly fear, though He was a Son, yet He learned obedience by the things which He suffered. And having been perfected, He became the author of eternal salvation to all who obey Him, called by God as High Priest "according to the order of Melchizedek,"* (Hebrews 5:7-10)

Jesus Christ is a good example of what we are speaking about. We know He was the unblemished and spotless Lamb of God.

> *but with the precious blood of Christ, as of a lamb without blemish and without spot.* (1 Peter 1:19)

Jesus Christ did not need an offering for His sin because He did not have any sin. In that sense, He is what we are once the blood of Jesus Christ has been sprinkled over us. Yet, Jesus Christ still had to achieve perfection or completion, which was the completion of

His purpose. For this, He needed the grace of heaven. So do we. After we are perfected in our relationship with God, we need to go on to perfection in our purpose for God. You were not just created for salvation from hell, but you were created and chosen for good works through the power of the Christ!

> *For by grace you have been saved through faith, and that not of yourselves; it is the gift of God, not of works, lest anyone should boast. For we are His workmanship, created in Christ Jesus for good works, which God prepared beforehand that we should walk in them.* (Ephesians 2:8-10)

As we pursue the purpose God has for us, His purpose to be conformed to the image of Christ is accomplished in us. God uses the choices and circumstances of our calling to form us in person and character. It is through this process we become conformed to the image and likeness of Christ. This causes what God has done in the inner man to become fully integrated with our natural man, making us the new creation He has called us to be. This is the time for the new creation to come forth. The power of God will flow through us according to how we let Him work in us!

> *Now to Him who is able to do exceedingly abundantly above all that we ask or think, according to the power that works in us, to Him be glory in the church by Christ Jesus to all generations, forever and ever. Amen.* (Ephesians 3:20-21)

This is the day when the glory of the Lord will be revealed, and all flesh shall see it together. Are you ready and willing to allow this glory to be revealed in your life?

Since the things of God seem so improbable before they happen, we often have difficulty receiving the new thing God is bringing to the church. One day Jesus Christ made a declaration to His disciples about the church. He said, *"I will build my church."* We have been emphasizing the ongoing unfolding of God's plan for the ages, and we need to see this is also true in church history. Jesus Christ started something, and it has been moving forward ever since. The Scriptures are clear; it has been an increasing kingdom since the time of its inception.

> *For unto us a Child is born, Unto us a Son is given; And the government will be upon His shoulder. And His name will be called Wonderful, Counselor, Mighty God, Everlasting Father, Prince of Peace. Of the increase of His government and peace There will be no end, Upon the throne of David and over His kingdom, To order it and establish it with judgment and justice From that time forward, even forever. The zeal of the Lord of hosts will perform this.* (Isaiah 9:6-7)

Jesus Christ was the seed of the new era. He would sprout, preach, and demonstrate the message of the kingdom of God. As a part of this process, He would also die, be buried, and rise from the dead. From a natural perspective, His arrest and crucifixion seemed like a defeat or at least a temporary setback. But we know this was not the case. It was all part of God's original plan. What often looks like a setback to us is never one from God's perspective. We need to begin to see history from God's perspective and not our own.

This is also true when we speak about the concept of restoration. When we hear about God's restoration, we look at it from the wrong point of view. The concept of restoration is quite different with a biblical perspective rather than with a human one. Our idea of restoration is that something has fallen apart so it needs to be brought back to what it was. This is incorrect. From God's perspective, He is restoring the spiritual and prophetic reality, not the natural one. This is why the children of Israel struggled so much when they came out of Babylon and returned to Jerusalem to be a part of God's great restoration. They looked at everything from a natural perspective. In this natural perspective, they continually struggled with God and the leadership God had placed over them. Because they were looking back from a natural perspective, they couldn't enjoy the wonderful spiritual reality of the time.

In the seventh month, on the twenty-first of the month, the word of the LORD came by Haggai the prophet, saying: "Speak now to Zerubbabel the son of Shealtiel, governor of Judah, and to Joshua the son of Jehozadak, the high priest, and to the remnant of the people, saying: 'Who is left among you who saw this temple in its former glory? And how do you see it now? In comparison with it, is this not in your eyes as nothing? (Haggai 2:1-3)

From the natural perspective, things were looking badly because this present building did not at all demonstrate the glory of the past to them. God is a progressive God, and things will look differently because they are moving forward. To see this, you must have a spiritual perspective. This is the role of the prophetic voice. Prophets bring a spiritual and godly perspective to what seems like human failure.

'According to the word that I covenanted with you when you came out of Egypt, so My Spirit remains among you; do not fear!' "For thus says the LORD of hosts: 'Once more (it is a little while) I will shake heaven and earth, the sea and dry land; and I will shake all nations, and they shall come to the Desire of All Nations, and I will fill this temple with glory,' says the LORD of hosts. 'The silver is Mine, and the gold is Mine,' says the LORD of hosts. 'The glory of this latter temple shall be greater than the former,' says the LORD of hosts. 'And in this place I will give peace,' says the LORD of hosts." (Haggai 2:5-9)

God is always taking us to a greater glory, but we often fail to understand or see what God is doing. *"Believe His prophets and you shall prosper,"* says the Word of God. This is possible because we are not looking from a human perspective but from God's. God is not restoring human institutions, but God is restoring what He has spoken prophetically beginning in the book of Genesis chapter three. In Acts it tells us:

> *Repent therefore and be converted, that your sins may be*
> *blotted out, so that times of refreshing may come from the*
> *presence of the Lord, and that He may send Jesus Christ, who*
> *was preached to you before, whom heaven must receive until*
> *the times of restoration of all things, which God has spoken*
> *by the mouth of all His holy prophets since the world began.*
> (Acts 3:19-21)

Notice it says: the restoration of all things spoken of by the prophets from the foundation of the world. The first prophetic declaration of God is the foretelling of the victory of the seed of the woman over the serpent in Genesis chapter 3.

The Bible says Abraham, the father of our faith, believed in the God who called the things that were not as though they were. The true reality for the person of faith is not the natural world we see but the world God declares it to be! The people of faith, the people of the kingdom of God, see the reality of the spiritual kingdom. We accept the declaration of Jesus Christ: *"the kingdom of God is at hand."*

An example of how this works is the restoration of the tabernacle of David as was prophesied by the prophet Amos.

> *"On that day I will raise up The tabernacle of David, which*
> *has fallen down, And repair its damages; I will raise up its*
> *ruins, And rebuild it as in the days of old;* (Amos 9:11)

David had built a tabernacle for the presence of God in the time before the building of the Temple by Solomon. He had established an order of praise and worship to minister before the Lord there. David's tabernacle did not have the three distinct courts after the pattern of Moses and the future temple of Solomon. His tabernacle was a picture of the immediate access people could have to the presence of God. When the prophet spoke of the rebuilding or raising up again of the tabernacle, you would have missed God if you thought this was a natural event. In the New Testament, the early church realized this was actually a picture of the tearing down of the walls of separation between the Jews and the Gentiles. It represented the opening of God's salvation to all the nations of the earth.

And after they had become silent, James answered, saying, "Men and brethren, listen to me: Simon has declared how God at the first visited the Gentiles to take out of them a people for His name. And with this the words of the prophets agree, just as it is written: 'After! this I will return And will rebuild the tabernacle of David, which has fallen down; I will rebuild its ruins, And I will set it up; So that the rest of mankind may seek the LORD, Even all the Gentiles who are called by My name, Says the LORD who does all these things.' (Acts 15:13-17)

Although in one sense this was a time of restoration as they were returning to their land and rebuilding the ruins of the past, they needed to see from a spiritual perspective. The spiritual perspective is that even when it looks like a restoration, God is actually adding something along the way. It is not a restoration in the natural sense but restoration to God's original intent. It is a part of the process of building from God's perspective. If what they had before was good enough, it would have lasted. What God builds will last; it is only the work of man that will fade or need restoration. What God is building not only needs parts added but there is also the removing of the fleshly parts we have contributed. In the process of removing flesh, we think things are going backward. Once you understand flesh does not glory in God's sight, you can see progress when the flames come to burn away the works of flesh.

For no other foundation can anyone lay than that which is laid, which is Jesus Christ. Now if anyone builds on this foundation with gold, silver, precious stones, wood, hay, straw, each one's work will become clear; for the Day will declare it, because it will be revealed by fire; and the fire will test each one's work, of what sort it is. (1 Corinthians 3:11-13)

We are living in the time when once again God is shaking everything that can be shaken. The systems of this world will fall. We cannot nor should we try to redeem them. But we should grab hold of the promises of God and begin to see the reality of the kingdom of God arising in the earth and the mighty sons of the kingdom of God rising up in the church! Are you ready to reveal the glory of God to your world? Hear the prophetic word and act upon it by faith.

> *Arise, shine; For your light has come! And the glory of the LORD is risen upon you. For behold, the darkness shall cover the earth, And deep darkness the people; But the LORD will arise over you, And His glory will be seen upon you. The Gentiles shall come to your light, And kings to the brightness of your rising.* (Isaiah 60:1-3)

The things I have written in this book, especially our natural and spiritual development as a progressive walk drawing us closer to the plan and purpose of God for our life, may seem to be impossible. But I close with the ultimate hope. The hope we have is the understanding that, in the end, it is about what God is doing. It is about what He is able to do, not us. It is the understanding that He created us to be the hope of the world He created. How can we fail?

> *What then shall we say to these things? If God is for us, who can be against us? He who did not spare His own Son, but delivered Him up for us all, how shall He not with Him also freely give us all things? Who shall bring a charge against God's elect? It is God who justifies. Who is he who condemns? It is Christ who died, and furthermore is also risen, who is even at the right hand of God, who also makes intercession for us. Who shall separate us from the love of Christ? Shall tribulation, or distress, or persecution, or*

famine, or nakedness, or peril, or sword? As it is written: "For Your sake we are killed all day long; We are accounted as sheep for the slaughter." Yet in all these things we are more than conquerors through Him who loved us. (Romans 8:31-37)

Notes

Notes

Notes

Other Books by Loren Covarrubias

ABOUT FATHER'S HOUSE

Today is the appointed time when God will exalt His house! He has given the church the responsibility for building the temple of His glory. But we must learn to submit in obedience, fully confident in the Father's plan, because anything genuine and lasting must first proceed from Him.

About Father's House is a powerful and inspiring look at the heart of the Father for His church. It shows how the local church is a witness and testimony of His covenant with the earth. Learn how you can mature from a servant, to a friend, to a son and full heir of God. This book will minister to your spirit and stir your vision to see the church brought to her rightful place of exaltation.

> *"Now it shall come to pass in the latter days that the mountain of the LORD's house shall be established on the top of the mountains, and shall be exalted above the hills; and all nations shall flow to it."* (Isaiah 2:2)

DISCOVERING FAVOR WITH GOD

This book is full of good news and real possibilities. You will discover what you have always wanted—God's favor and the daily experience of His presence and care. God's favor is closer than most of us can imagine; it is not so elusive or selective as some would have you believe. Destiny is at humanity's doorstep, your doorstep, thanks to God's favor.

In *Discovering Favor with God,* you will learn how to:
- Experience the favor of God in your daily life.
- Enjoy the intimacy of Daddy's lap as well as the destiny of Father's purpose.
- Deal with the devils in your own garden.
- Discover life in another dimension. You are about to discover and experience what you have always desired—the favor of God.

Other Books by Loren Covarrubias continued

WHY IS THE DEVIL IN MY GARDEN?

At a young age we typically have planted in our minds the idea of the devil as a little figure in a red suit with a tail carrying a pitchfork. He is someone to fear because he is "out to get us." As we grow older we realize that the devil probably doesn't look like that, but there is still a visual picture that comes to mind when the devil is mentioned and we most definitely keep the idea that the devil is "out to get us."

Where did the myth of the devil in a red suit with a pitchfork come from? It really doesn't matter but it shows us how easy it is to get something planted in our minds that has no apparent origin and seems to do no harm to us.

Much of what people believe about the devil is based upon subjective experiences and traditions rather than the Word of God. While it may appear that it doesn't matter what we believe concerning the devil, we need to understand that when we comprehend the role of the devil in the plan of God, we can more effectively resist him.

This book will challenge your beliefs about the devil and the role he plays both in the world and in your own personal life. Some of the questions that will be addressed may shake the core of your belief about the forces of evil and the ways to fight the devil, but I am confident that if you will examine the scriptures with me you will see what the Word of God tells us concerning these things.